The Path to a Stress-Free Retirement

Your blueprint for building a personal paycheck for life

The Path to a Stress-Free Retirement

Copyright © 2019 by Patrick T. Lyman

All rights reserved. No part of this publication may be reproduced, distributed, or transmitted in any form or by any means, including photocopying, recording, or other electronic or mechanical methods, without the prior written permission of the publisher or copyright holder, except in the case of brief quotations embodied in critical reviews and certain other noncommercial uses permitted by copyright law.

All information contained in this book is subject to change. This book should not be considered a substitute for legal, tax, or financial advice. This book makes no offers or guarantees of coverage, asset performance, or income to readers.

Patrick T. Lyman, CAS, CSA, RFC, RHU

This book is dedicated most importantly to my wife, Marti, and our three children, Kristen, Colin, and Geoff, their spouses, Brendon, Beckie, and Kelly and my grandkids Evan, Preston, Erynn, and Landen. The love, support, and encouragement of my family along the way helped make a challenging project just a little easier.

I would also like to add a special dedication to my late mother-in-law, Sylvia. She proved beyond a shadow of a doubt that with discipline, patience, foresight, and willingness to take sound financial advice, you can create a realistic income plan that will last not only as long as you live, but one that can also continue on throughout the lives of your children and grandchildren. A true legacy.

Thanks, Mom. We will never forget you!

The Path to a Stress-Free Retirement

Patrick T. Lyman, CAS, CSA, RFC, RHU

PRAISE FOR

The Path to a Stress-Free Retirement

"*The Path to a Stress-Free Retirement* is very informative and easy to understand. I would recommend it to anyone who has questions about retirement, no matter what stage of planning they are in. This concise book made income and distribution planning more doable, using a step-by-step approach with different suggestions. I wish I had this book before I retired!" --Diane DiFrancesco

"Most of us are so focused on saving for retirement that we haven't even thought about how our nest egg will hopefully allow us to live comfortably the rest of our lives. *The Path to a Stress-Free Retirement* is a tool that helps change our mindset. Even if you're already retired, the book has tips and suggestions proving that it's not too late to change your game plan and maximize your retirement income." --Chris D. Scanzaroli

"There are countless books written today that focus on retirement planning. Many are either oversimplified or they speak in an industry language that the average reader does not understand. The Path to a Stress-Free Retirement is a great, comprehensive book that will be an asset to anyone regardless of their financial prowess. I highly recommend this book to anyone who is either currently building their nest egg or even nearing retirement." --Steve Tepfenhart, Advisor Development Consultant

Patrick T. Lyman, CAS, CSA, RFC, RHU

Table of Contents

Introduction 11

A Distribution Plan That Lasts 11

Using This Book 14

Personalizing Your Retirement Distribution Plan 15

Chapter 1 Your Retirement Planning Foundation 17

Accumulation 17

Protection 25

Distribution 27

Why Accumulation, Protection, and Distribution Are So Critical 28

Chapter 2 Transforming a Distribution Mindset to an Income Mindset 29

Income: A Better Thought Process for Planning 30

A Simple Blueprint for an Income Plan 33

Chapter 3 Threats to Adequate Retirement Income ... 35

    Market Risk 35

    Longevity Risk 36

    Health 37

    Interest Rates 38

    Inflation 38

Taxes 39

Poor Planning 40

Chapter 4 Creating Your Stress-Free Retirement Income Plan 43

Figuring Out How Much Income You Need When You Retire 44

Postretirement Income Needs Assessment 45

Tips for Income Planning 49

Avoiding the Traps of Old Planning Wisdom 50

Chapter 5 The Value of Guarantees 57

Guarantees versus Fixed Interest 58

Guarantees versus Projections 59

Guarantees and Accumulation: The Secret of an Annuity 61

A Closer Look at Fixed Index Annuities 67

   FIAs vs. the Stock Market 67

Chapter 6 Finding the Right Pension and Social Security Elections 73

Introducing Clive and Sarah 73

Let's Meet Luke and Ann 75

At What Age Should YOU Take Social Security? 76

Breaking Even 79

Pension Options 80

Chapter 7 Inheritance and Income Planning 83

The Reality of Inheritance 83
The Emotional Dynamics of Inheritance 86
The Practicalities 87
    Requesting Funds 88
What to Do with an Inheritance 91
From Inheritance to Income 93
Talking about Inheritance 95

Chapter 8 Your Paycheck for Life: Customizing Your Income Plan 99
Self-Assessment 99
Putting It All Together 102
Jon and Hope 106
Peter and Laura 107
Kate and Andrew 108

Chapter 9 Carving Out Your Legacy and Estate Planning 113
Life Insurance 114
Annuities 115
Investments 116

Conclusion 121
Glossary 123
Acknowledgments 127
About the Author 129

The Path to a Stress-Free Retirement

Patrick T. Lyman, CAS, CSA, RFC, RHU

Introduction

A Distribution Plan That Lasts

"How long will my retirement savings last?" That's a question too many retirees are forced to consider before they pull the trigger on leaving work or reducing hours to enjoy their golden years. After spending all or most of their working life struggling to save money for retirement, they're left struggling with a new kind of financial security right at the time when they're supposed to be able to enjoy themselves and start checking off boxes on their bucket lists.

Imagine you and your spouse retiring at age 65 with $500,000 saved. It sounds like a lot—but it's probably going to have to last you both at least 20 years. Not only that, but couples who are 65 can take $285,000 off the top for medical expenses.[1] So now, less than half of what you

---

[1] Fidelity Benefits Consulting estimate; https://www.fidelity.com/bin-public/060_www_fidelity_com/documents/press-release/healthcare-

originally saved has to last you and your spouse 20 years—and don't be surprised to see that number rise over the coming years. That's just $10,750 in principal each year you can pull out from your retirement savings to live on, if you have it invested in bonds or CDs growing at 1 to 2 percent, if you have no investment losses, and if you can reinvest each of these fixed investments at the same rate once they mature. That's a lot of ifs.

I don't want to be all doom and gloom about this, but the statistics say we really have no choice. Consider that:

- The median amount saved by those between the ages of 64 and 75 is nowhere near the $500,000 used in our example above but is just $126,000.[2]
- Forty-two percent of Americans expect to retire with less than $10,000 saved.[3]
- Most adults aged 65 to 74 spend more than $48,000 a year on food, transportation, and other living expenses.[4]
- Housing costs alone cost the average 65-and-up senior $1,322 per month.[5]

price-check-040219.pdf

[2] https://www.cnbc.com/2018/03/19/most-americans-close-to-retirement-have-saved-12-percent-of-what-they-need.html

[3] https://www.marketwatch.com/story/now-the-bad-news-and-slightly-less-horrible-news-about-saving-for-retirement-2018-03-07

[4] https://www.bls.gov/opub/btn/volume-5/spending-patterns-of-older-americans.htm

[5] https://www.nerdwallet.com/blog/investing/could-you-survive-for-23-years-on-your-savings/

Of course, there are things that seniors can do to improve their odds of having a successful retirement and making their savings last. Many of the tips we see out there advise us to retire later, work part-time after retirement, and get more aggressive with savings in our final working years.

These are all great tips, and they can definitely help increase the amount you have saved, but they still don't address the issue of ensuring that your savings last for however long you're retired.

It doesn't matter where you are in your retirement planning, whether you're just now getting started or you're on the cusp of retiring from a lifetime career. Even if you think you're never going to totally retire—whatever your stage in life, you need to make room in your process for thinking about not just retirement savings accumulation but retirement savings distribution and how you can best plan for distribution that lasts a lifetime.

It's for this purpose that I wrote this book, which can easily be used in conjunction with any of my other books in the Retirement Planning series.

Using This Book

In writing this book, I wanted to make sure I gave readers a workable action plan with which to move forward. That way, you won't just have the concept of distribution planning mastered but you'll also have the tools you need to put a real plan in place, a direction from which to start, and a solution to start maximizing your retirement savings.

To that end, I've included a checklist at the end of every chapter. The checklist isn't an assignment that you must do, but it will include relevant steps from the chapter that give you a starting point for implementing whatever strategy has been discussed.

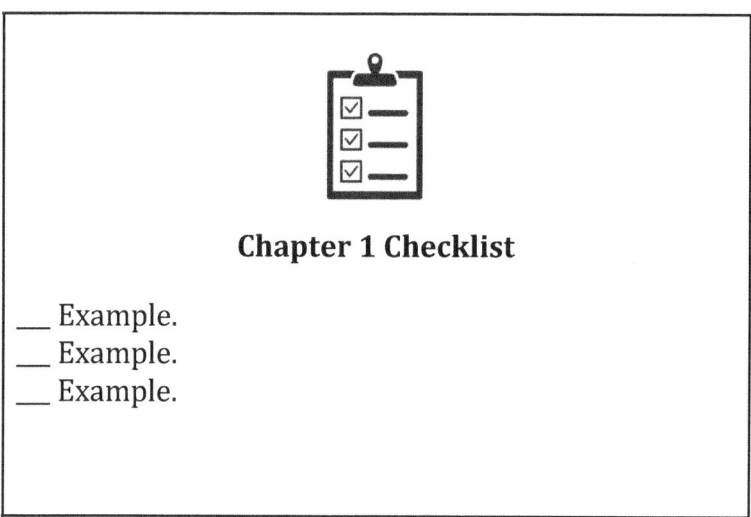

Chapter 1 Checklist

__ Example.
__ Example.
__ Example.

I've also added some specific tips throughout the book to help people in certain phases of their retirement journey. The tips I've included will help:

Retired
Already relying on savings and/or Social Security

Patrick T. Lyman, CAS, CSA, RFC, RHU

> **Soon to retire**
> Retiring in the next 10 years

> **Under 55 or not planning to retire**
> For those who don't plan to retire, or younger savers who want income planning tips after reading the *30-Day Retirement Plan*

Personalizing Your Retirement Distribution Plan

The last thing I want is for any reader to walk away from this book thinking that there's only one right way to plan their retirement distribution. There are many options you can explore, depending on your overall retirement plans, the amount you've been able to save, and your personal risk tolerance.

There's no need to enter a plan that doesn't suit your personal needs. This book is all about giving you options to mix and match that can help you personalize your retirement distribution and enjoy the senior years you've been dreaming of.

The Path to a Stress-Free Retirement

Patrick T. Lyman, CAS, CSA, RFC, RHU

Chapter 1

Your Retirement Planning Foundation

In this book, I will focus primarily on distribution planning, but before we get into the nitty-gritty, I want to talk about the three most critical elements of complete retirement planning. It takes all of these planning phases to be properly implemented before you can create a thorough and secure retirement plan. Let's look at each of these phases on its own, and then talk about why this trio is so critical.

Accumulation

Accumulation is the part of retirement planning that revolves around growing the value of your retirement account(s). One of the primary methods of accumulation is saving money. Creating a budget that minimizes spending and maximizes saving is a great place to start. Part of accumulation is also choosing where to put your money. Whenever you contribute to an IRA, 401(k), 403(b), or other retirement savings account, you're accumulating funds for the future in a tax-favored way, which gives you added advantages either before or after you retire. When your employer pays their 401(k) match or makes a deposit into a retirement account on your behalf, that too is accumulation.

Another component of accumulation is investing. To save as much as you'll need for retirement, accumulation has to be about more than just stockpiling savings and sitting on the cash. Not only does earning interest and investment returns on your savings help accelerate your accumulation, but with the proper investments and accounts chosen, your interest can compound, meaning that you earn interest and returns on both your interest and principal. When your interest isn't compounding and only your principal is growing, it's considered simple interest.

To see how these two approaches to interest payments differ, let's look at how the value of a $1,000,000 investment can grow when it's getting simple interest of 1.5 percent over 25 years. See Figure 1 and 2 on the following pages.

Simple Interest

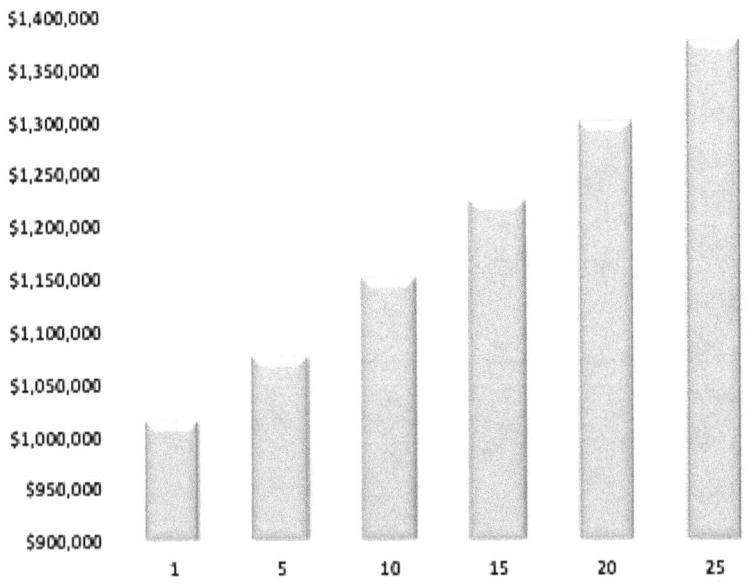

FIGURE 1

Initial Investment	$1,000,000
Annual Interest	1.50%
Year	Balance
1	$1,015,000
5	$1,075,000
10	$1,150,000
15	$1,225,000
20	$1,300,000
25	$1,375,000

FIGURE 2

Now, in Figures 3 and 4, let's look at the same amount growing at 1.5 percent interest that's compounding.

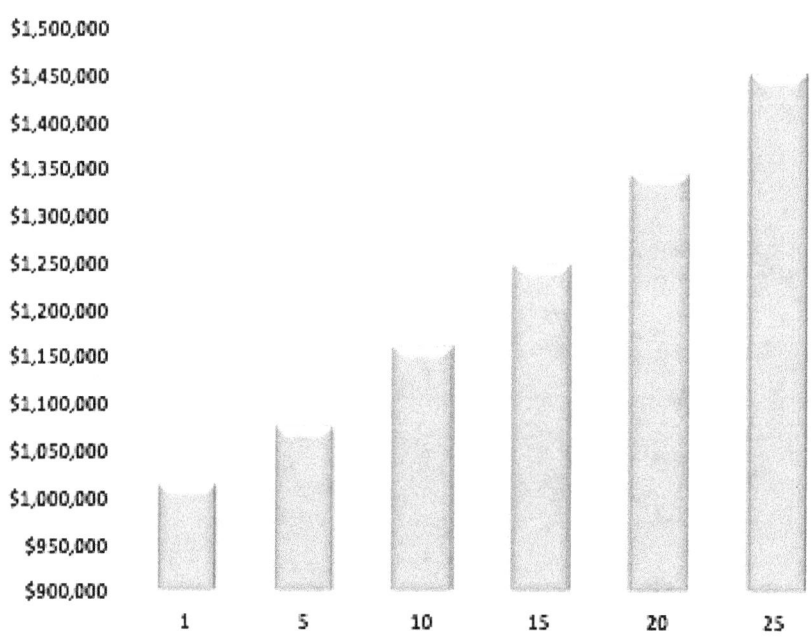

FIGURE 3

Initial Investment	$1,000,000
Annual Interest	1.50%
Year	Balance
1	$1,015,000
5	$1,077,284
10	$1,160,541
15	$1,250,232
20	$1,346,855
25	$1,450,945

FIGURE 4

An interest rate of 1.5 percent might not sound like much, but if you look at Figure 4, you can see that the compounded gains are more than $450,000 at that rate. The simple interest growth isn't as good, but it still hits $375,000, which is significant.

Now, in Figures 5 and 6, let's look at a direct comparison of the growth with simple and compound interest to truly understand the difference.

The Path to a Stress-Free Retirement

SIMPLE INTEREST VERSUS COMPOUND INTEREST

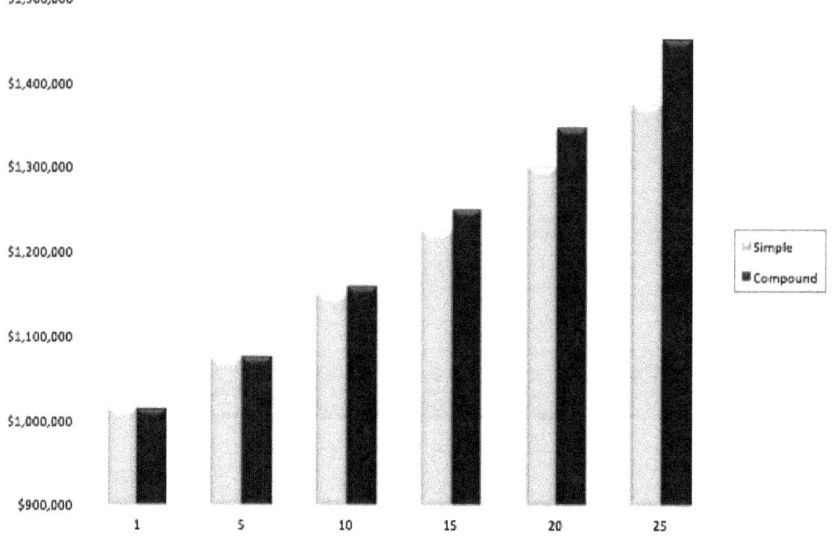

FIGURE 5

Initial Investment	$1,000,000	
Annual Interest	1.50%	
Year	Balance (simple)	Balance (compound)
1	$1,015,000	$1,015,000
5	$1,075,000	$1,077,284
10	$1,150,000	$1,160,541
15	$1,225,000	$1,250,232
20	$1,300,000	$1,346,855
25	$1,375,000	$1,450,945

FIGURE 6

As you can see, making sure your savings are compounding for as long as possible is critical to your overall accumulation plan and success.

In the early years, many savers will invest more aggressively in stocks and other largely volatile investments. While these can involve a higher risk of loss, they also have the opportunity for more aggressive returns, and it's important to have those returns in the early years since they can compound, as illustrated in Figure 3. It's also a more prudent strategy to expose yourself to potential losses while you're still working because then you can save more and compensate for the losses, making them much easier to recover from than they would be after you retire.

In later years, as working hours wind down, savers generally focus on moving their assets to lower-risk, fixed-interest or income investments such as annuities, bonds, and money markets. These may have a lower potential for returns than stocks, but they also have less risk of loss, which is vital to someone getting closer to retirement.

Retired

Even though you're retired and your income is reduced, you still need to focus on building, protecting, and maintaining some growth so that your money can keep pace with inflation. But you can no longer absorb the risk of allocating significant funds to the stock market.

Instead, think about a more conservative accumulation strategy, such as laddered CDs. This is a strategy in which you invest in multiple CDs with varying maturity dates. Other considerations can include extremely conservative bond funds and tax-exempt municipal bond funds for nonretirement assets.

You shouldn't get crazy with growth possibilities once you've retired, but you do want to maintain some conservative growth.

Soon to retire

As someone who's still working but nearing retirement age, your first priority is to adjust your budget so that you can deposit every extra dollar you have into your retirement accounts. Make sure you're maxing out any employer contributions, that you're making any catch-up contributions you're entitled to, and that you're considering postretirement tax ramifications of all your accounts.

Soon to retire

When you're about five years out from retirement, it's a good idea to dial down to a more conservative portfolio and focus on conservative growth that doesn't subject your principal to a lot of unnecessary risk. You might want to look into growth and income annuities, which we'll talk more about in Chapter 5.

> **Under 55 or not planning to retire**
>
> You may be decades away from retirement, or not planning to retire at all, but if you want to protect your savings, then you still have work to do. Generally speaking, you want to build and maintain a portfolio that's consistent with your risk tolerance, which means consistently rebalancing as the value of your investments change. You also want to properly diversify, focusing on a variety of investment vehicles including stocks, bonds, money markets, mutual funds, index funds, and annuities.
>
> For those who are in their 30s and 40s, consider an allocation mix that's 60 percent equities and 40 percent bonds and annuities, which are essentially equivalent to having money in a bond portfolio but with more upside potential and no risk of loss.

Protection

Saving money is a start, but if you don't protect the money you've saved and grown, then you still won't have anything to rely on in retirement. That's why, as discussed in the last section, savers move to less risky investments as they age—because they want to protect the funds they've accumulated. To do this, they might focus on lower-risk investments such as bonds and CDs, or investments with guarantees like annuities.

Protecting your money is about more than being a more conservative investor as you age, however. It's also about reducing your overall financial risk through insurance. With insurance to protect your home, your life, your car, your liabilities, your business, your health, your income, and your potential long-term care needs, you ensure that disasters like car accidents, house fires, job losses, and illnesses don't force you to take funds out of your retirement accounts to stay solvent before you've even retired.

Retired

You may think that you no longer need insurance for long-term care once you get Medicare, but remember that Medicare doesn't cover expenses related to assistance with activities of daily living. If you're ever in need of help with tasks like eating, bathing, and dressing, Medicare isn't likely to pay.

Soon to retire

Now is not the time to give up your disability insurance. Instead, make sure you maintain that coverage until you no longer have a regular income to lose, which can be up to age 70, assuming you are still working at that time.

Under 55 or not planning to retire

Even if you don't plan to retire, you need to protect your assets as if you do. Medical emergencies, economic changes, and unexpected chronic illnesses can force you into retirement even if you don't want

> them to. That means you need to have your assets ready to provide an income, whether you intend to take it or not.

Distribution

The final element of retirement planning basically undoes everything you've done so far. It's all about taking funds out of your retirement accounts so you can supplement other income (like Social Security or pension benefits) and pay your living expenses.

Some of your distributions will be used to help you maintain regular monthly expenses. Some may be used to fund an emergency expense, such as replacing a broken appliance. Others might be used to buy a special gift, to fulfill a bucket-list wish, or to go on a trip. Whatever you take money out for, the point is that your distribution phase is all about accessing the funds you've accumulated and protected.

This is an enjoyable phase, but it's a stage where a lot of devastating mistakes can be made, and too few people talk or warn about them before it's too late. The thing is, accumulation and protection don't have to stop or get thrown by the wayside while you're in the distribution phase. In fact, if you want to avoid becoming broke in retirement, it's vital you learn how to create a distribution plan that honors an ongoing commitment to accumulation and protection. Otherwise, your distribution phase is going to be more of a depletion phase.

Why Accumulation, Protection, and Distribution Are So Critical

A three-legged stool or table can't stand on two legs alone. The same is true of your retirement plan. There is no plan if there are no savings or no accumulation. And there's no point in accumulating if you aren't going to protect what you're saving. The goal of both of those moves is to help you get to a point where you can distribute the funds you've saved and ensure a comfortable lifestyle throughout your retirement years.

Chapter 1 Checklist

__ Document some of your objectives and plans for accumulation.

__ Document some of your objectives and plans for protection.

__ Document some of your objectives and plans for distribution.

Patrick T. Lyman, CAS, CSA, RFC, RHU

Chapter 2

Transforming a Distribution Mindset to an Income Mindset

When it comes to retirement planning, people are understandably preoccupied with accumulation and principal protection. Many assume that if they just save enough and hold on to it, they won't have anything to worry about once they leave work. After all, we know, and the media never fails to tell us, that if we don't save enough and we don't hold on to our savings, we will have no funds to use to maintain our lifestyles upon retirement.

But the money you save, whether it's $100,000 or $1,000,000, is a finite resource. As you spend it, your balances are going to fall and you're going to run out of money, no matter what that online retirement calculator told you.

This single-minded focus on savings does a lot more damage than you might think. Because it doesn't give seniors and preretirees knowledge of the tools they need to use to handle ongoing distributions from their savings, it leaves them far more likely to either withdraw too much, putting their financial security in peril, or to withdraw too little, forcing them to live well below their means and possibly reduce their quality of life for no reason.

But there is a better way—and it starts by creating a retirement income plan.

Income: A Better Thought Process for Planning

During your working years, you exchange your time and effort for a paycheck at regular intervals. With this paycheck, you can easily budget your expenses and time your bill payments to make sure your overall spending stays within the limits of what your paycheck affords you. As long as your employer is dependable, you have relatively little stress that you could suddenly be without a paycheck, and you can focus on the day-to-day responsibilities you have rather than fretting over where your next month's cash is going to come from and whether you'll still have cash available six months from now.

Once you're retired, however, you no longer have those dependable paychecks stretching out in front of you. Instead, you have the full balance of all your retirement accounts, ready for you to access at will. There is no one there to issue you these funds at regular intervals to force you to stay on a certain budget, and you have no guarantee that the funds will remain available so that you can continue to pay them out to yourself as needed in the years and decades to come.

Social Security and pension payments give you some idea of what it's like to continue having a paycheck after you retire, but they may not be enough. If you're receiving a Social Security benefit of $1,500 a month, then you know every month you're getting that $1,500 for the rest of your life and you can budget yourself within those confines. But when you need $3,000 a month to live, and when emergencies crop up requiring extra cash, Social Security falls short and it's up to you to fill the role of income distributor.

But how can you guarantee yourself an income 10 or 20 years into the future when you don't know how economic changes could impact your savings, how inflation could impact your spending needs, and whether medical expenses could deplete your retirement accounts?

The goal of changing your retirement savings thought process and to develop an income mindset is to create a situation where you're getting your retirement savings distributed regularly as an income NO MATTER WHAT, just like your Social Security and pension. It's to remove the financial instability and insecurity that can come with managing your own postretirement distribution plan and ensure that you turn your savings into an ongoing, guaranteed source of income for your whole retirement.

> **Retired**
> It's not too late to take what's left in your savings and rework your retirement plan to focus on income. Start looking at income objectives, needs, expectations, and shortfalls. Then, start looking at products such as annuities with income guarantees (discussed in detail in Chapter 5), bonds, CDs, and dividend stocks to see how an assortment of these vehicles can create the steady income you need.

> **Soon to retire**
> This is an ideal spot to be in for planning income because all your savings are still available. As you dial down risk exposure so you're not putting retirement savings in jeopardy, consider how much income you need, what sources of income you'll have, and what investment vehicles will help you create a guaranteed income stream when you retire.

> **Under 55 or not planning to retire**
> There are advantageous planning measures you can incorporate, even if you aren't retiring, that will still give you an income if your plans change. First, you can consider cash value life insurance as an additional source of guaranteed income at retirement as well as legacy protection. This is especially smart for younger savers because you can get good rates when you're young, something that will not be true as you age and

> your health changes.
>
> In addition, you can look at newer annuity products that offer guaranteed income, opportunities to grow principal, and have hybrid benefits so you can use them to pay for things like long-term care.

A Simple Blueprint for an Income Plan

When you're trying to save for retirement, you generally come up with a strategy. You work on your budget to lower expenses and ensure you can save as much as you've been advised you'll need. You max out your employer's 401(k) or 403(b), you strategize over taxable and nontaxable accounts, you invest and rebalance and so on.

When you plan your postretirement *income*, you take part in a similar process of maximizing and strategizing. Some of the issues you should consider in your income plan include:

- **Threats to retirement income:** This includes how things like market risk and inflation can impact your retirement income and how to plan around them.
- **Reassessing standard retirement formulas:** Entails determining whether standard advice like the 4 percent rule will work for you.
- **Looking for investment products with guarantees:** This is vital because guarantees of

distribution and earnings are essential in your income plan.
- **Making the right Social Security and pension elections:** This starts by taking into account your age, life expectancy, marital status, and more.
- **Ways to create a lifetime paycheck:** You won't have an employer to pay you, but with proper planning, you can write your own paycheck for life.
- **Legacy and inheritance planning:** Involves finding ways to ensure you leave a legacy and you maximize those legacies left to you.

Each of these issues will be discussed in more detail in later chapters.

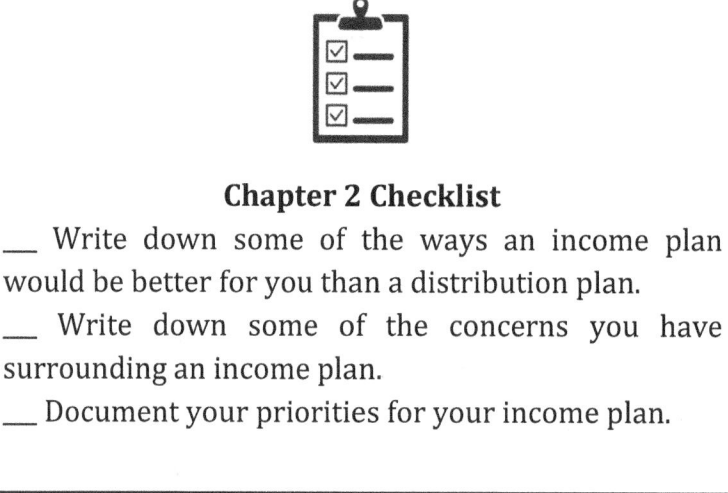

Chapter 2 Checklist

__ Write down some of the ways an income plan would be better for you than a distribution plan.

__ Write down some of the concerns you have surrounding an income plan.

__ Document your priorities for your income plan.

Patrick T. Lyman, CAS, CSA, RFC, RHU

Chapter 3

Threats to Adequate Retirement Income

No matter how careful you are while saving money, by the time your reach retirement and start using the funds you've saved, there are always income threats lurking. Let's look at some of the most common risks you're likely to encounter and talk about some ways you can protect your savings and income from them.

Market Risk

Any investment that's tied to a market (like the stock or bond market) carries an innate risk that it can lose value simply because the market it's tied to drops. For example, let's say you're carrying 100 shares of XYZ company stock. The company is doing great, it has high earnings, low debt, good management, an in-demand product, no competition, and so on. By all accounts, there's no reason its stock price should fall.

But then a major disaster strikes the United States or an economic disaster occurs, like the price of oil doubling overnight or the value of the dollar quickly dropping, and investors start getting scared. As a result, investors start to pull back, selling off stocks in every company, including XYZ, and the whole market plunges. This causes the price of XYZ to plummet, taking your portfolio value along with it.

This is a scary situation no matter when it happens, but imagine it's happening as you're in need of income. You're then forced to sell XYZ at this suppressed value and lock in your losses, rather than giving it time to come back.

One of the best ways to protect yourself from market risk is to make sure you have a well-diversified portfolio that ensures you have a variety of investments not all tied to the same markets. That way as one market falls, another might be rising, giving you some ongoing growth to offset losses and giving you alternative products to liquidate when you're in need.

Longevity Risk

I wouldn't be surprised if most people want to live long lives, or maybe even want to live forever. But there's a big problem with living 100 or more years, and it even affects people like billionaire Peter Theil, who has long been focused on ways to extend life.[6] The problem? Outliving the money you have saved.

A billion dollars, which is a thousand million, or $1,000,000,000, may seem like an unending sum, but if living forever was possible, having $1 billion would make a very small dent in overall lifetime expenses. Likewise, having $200,000 saved might not get you through a retirement that could last 20 or 30 years, unless you have the proper planning.

One way to fight back against longevity risk while still crossing your fingers at a long life is to focus your postretirement income strategy on products that offer a lifetime income guarantee, such as an annuity.

Health

No matter how healthy you are now, you might find yourself facing the expenses of chronic illness treatment as you age. Even if you don't, you can expect a big chunk of your postretirement income to go toward health expenses. As an example, according to HealthView Services, a healthy 55-year-old woman retiring at age 65 can expect to spend $13,165 per year on health expenses.[7]

It's never too late to start improving your health as a means of minimizing future expenses, a topic covered in far more detail in *Your 30-Day Retirement Plan*. Visit your doctor as often as recommended, get all your early health

---

[6]https://www.nytimes.com/2018/01/25/opinion/sunday/silicon-valley-immortality.html

[7]http://www.hvsfinancial.com/wp-content/uploads/2019/07/Health-in-Retirement-Planning.pdf

screenings, and talk to your doctor about a good diet and exercise plan for you to maintain.

Interest Rates

When you think about financial risks in retirement, interest rate risk might not come to mind immediately, but it should. As you age, you switch to more conservative investments, like multiyear guaranteed annuities, CDs, and bonds. Investments like these have a maturity date, at which time your principal can be reinvested in a new CD, bond, or other fixed investment.

If interest rates have fallen since you bought the now-matured investment, then you will reinvest that money at a lower interest rate, which means your future growth won't meet your past growth. If you'd been relying on that interest as income, then it can also reduce your income moving forward.

One way to reduce your exposure to interest rate risk is to focus on laddered investments. When you do, it means you take one sum of money and invest it into several different CDs, annuities, or bonds with varying maturity dates, rather than taking the full lump sum and investing it into a single product. This allows you to keep some money invested in higher interest, older products and ensures you'll have new principal available once interest rates rise again.

Inflation

If you've been grocery shopping or buying gas for a decade or more, then you've noticed that the prices of general goods and services usually trends up over the years. This is the impact of inflation, and there's no getting around it. Inflation will continue into your retirement, with conservative estimates telling us we can expect the price of goods and services to rise an average 3.22 percent per year.[8] That means that roughly every two decades, prices on the goods and services you need will double.

Social Security often makes cost-of-living adjustments (COLA) to help seniors deal with rising costs, but it's also important to maintain some growth in your savings. Ideally, you want them to grow at least enough to keep up with inflation. In part, this is because you don't know how big or small the COLA increase might be. For example, in 2019, the COLA increase was 2.8 percent. But at the time of this writing, the 2020 COLA increase is estimated to be just 1.6 percent, which will ultimately create a $24 monthly increase for the average beneficiary.[9]

Still, whether it's a 2.8 percent increase or a 1.6 percent increase, it's not necessarily enough to keep up with inflation.

Taxes

Retirement gives us a break from working, but it doesn't give us a break from paying taxes. Every year, just as you did while working, you have to submit a tax return in retirement. This isn't so bad, unless you find out that you've got a huge tax bill to settle when you file.

---

[8] https://inflationdata.com/Inflation/Inflation_Rate/Long_Term_Inflation.asp

[9] https://www.ssa.gov/oact/cola/colaeffect.html

Avoiding that tax bill takes some preplanning. You want to watch the total amount of income you bring in from sources like part-time jobs, Social Security, and taxable accounts. You also want to make sure you have some sources of nontaxable income, such as municipal bonds and Roth retirement accounts.

I'm often asked by clients how they can minimize the amount of taxable income they have. I generally tell them that the key is to minimize what you're taking from taxable sources and focus instead on getting an income from nontaxable sources, such as Roth plans and annuities. No matter what, when you take distributions from a 401(k), 403(b), or non-Roth IRA, it's taxable. You've enjoyed a tax deduction and deferral for as long as you've owned the investment; when you start taking distributions, it's time to start paying taxes. Your required minimum distributions starting at age 72 (as of 2020) can't be delayed, except when they are from a 401(k) that you still contribute to with an employer you still work for.

Poor Planning

The threats covered on the prior pages are mostly outside your control. You don't dictate how low interest rates will go, whether the market will fall, how high taxes will go, how long you will live, how much inflation will impact your expenses, and so on. This does not mean you're completely powerless against protecting yourself from these risks, however, and that's really the central point of this section.

You are in control of your overall portfolio and income planning, which means you can minimize the risks you are exposed to and offset the damage they can do, as long as you take the necessary steps to conduct proper planning.

Proper planning starts with educating yourself, something you're doing with this book. But after you've been educated, you must take action to build safeguards into your portfolio so that you reduce your overall risk exposure and protect your income for life.

Retired

Even if you've been approaching postretirement spending informally and without a plan, it's not too late to be more deliberate about determining your income needs and creating a budget.

Soon to retire

This is a good time to review your existing portfolio to determine which allocations don't align with your risk tolerance and which ones do. Schedule regular reviews with your financial advisor as you get ready to retire.

Not planning to retire

Closely monitor your investment portfolio (401(k), 403(b), IRA, etc.) regularly to maximize growth potential while still working.

Chapter 3 Checklist

__ Make note of some of the risks you're especially concerned about or exposed to.

__ Create an account with the Social Security Administration to verify your potential benefits.

__ Start monitoring your investment portfolio more regularly.

Patrick T. Lyman, CAS, CSA, RFC, RHU

Chapter 4

Creating Your Stress-Free Retirement Income Plan

By this point, you may be thinking about retirement planning in a totally new way—one that positions income at the forefront. If this is a new concept for you, then it also might be causing some anxiety as you mentally revise your approach to include income planning.

The truth is, income planning doesn't have to be stressful. In fact, it's a relatively straightforward task that, once completed, lends itself to a much more secure and relaxed financial future. To get started, you just have to think about how much income you're going to need.

Figuring Out How Much Income You Need When You Retire

Whenever I talk to my clients about retirement planning, the question of how much income or savings they'll need during retirement always comes up. It's a complex question to address, because there are so many variables. The amount of debt you carry into retirement, your lifestyle needs and expectations, your marital status, your health, and your bucket list all factor in. Then, there are outside influences such as inflation and taxes that will have a bearing on your income needs, but it's impossible to know just how much.

You also need to consider all your potential sources of income. For example, if your Social Security and pension income are ample enough to cover all your expenses and lifestyle needs, you may not need an income from your savings. At least at first. As you age and your health or needs change, then you may find that you do.

Conventional wisdom tells us that we need to replace between 70 and 80 percent of our preretirement income while we're in retirement.[10] If you're looking for a basic rule of thumb, this is probably a pretty safe bet.

But if you want a more accurate number better tailored to your experience, ask yourself the following questions and consider the impact on your income needs that your answers will have.

---

[10] https://edis.ifas.ufl.edu/fy1355

Postretirement Income Needs Assessment

We'll kick off this needs assessment with determining your potential cost of living. To get there, answer the following questions.

Living expenses:
- What are the average expenses in the town/location/type of dwelling you want to live in at retirement?
- What are your insurance expenses?
- What are your anticipated utility expenses?
- What are your vehicle/transportation expenses?
- How much will you need for groceries?
- Will you have help cleaning, doing lawn maintenance, etc.? Will this help be seasonal or year-round?
- What will you need to set aside for home and vehicle maintenance?
- Will you still have debt to pay off in retirement?
- What banking/retirement account fees will you have?

Discretionary expenses:
- Do you plan to travel for fun?
- How much will you spend on hobbies (including books, periodicals, and cable)?
- How often do you plan to eat out?
- What classes might you attend?
- Will you travel to see family? How often?

- How often do you want to pay for personal grooming services?
- How often will you go shopping for:
    - clothes
    - housewares
    - linens
    - shoes
    - gadgets
    - home decor
    - gifts
    - collectibles
    - jewelry/watches
    - other: _____
    - other: _____
- How often will you seek out entertainment (movies, theater, concerts)?
- What memberships will you continue or start?

Into the future:
- What impact will inflation have on your income needs?
- How much of your postretirement income is taxable, and what might that look like/cost?
- Consider what portion of your Social Security income will be taxable based on your provisional income.
- Think about how much you can take out of your savings while not working and while maintaining a job. Compare the difference and the potential tax fallout to help you decide how long you might

ultimately need to work to make your money last longer.
- How will you handle the potential acceleration of medical expenses and long-term care?

After going through these questions, use your answers to come up with a ballpark budget for your postretirement lifestyle.

Next up, you need to consider the various nonsavings income sources you have to count on.

Potential sources of nonsavings income:
- Social Security for you and your spouse
- Pension benefits for you and your spouse
- Alimony
- Dividends
- Guaranteed income payments from annuities
- CD interest
- Bond interest
- Part-time or other work earnings
- Ongoing royalties
- Profit sharing

Add up these potential income totals.

Finally, you need to measure the shortfall between your anticipated expenses and your anticipated income. This gives you an idea of how much money you will have to pull

out of savings each year to close that gap. Now ask yourself:
- How long can your savings support your anticipated income needs?
- How much income could you get from lifetime guaranteed sources, such as annuities?
- How much additional income could you get from adding more bonds, CDs, and dividend stocks to your portfolio?
- What are some of the risks you're taking on with these products?
- How have you protected your principal and future income from these risks?

Retired

If you're already retired, you can approach this exercise using all your current expenses and investments, and assess how appropriate they are for your long-term needs. This will help you identify problem areas you need to change.

Soon to retire

You are in the ideal spot to do the assessment. Start researching alternative living arrangements and investments to better manage your postretirement income to ensure it's enough to fund a comfortable retirement.

> **Not planning to retire**
>
> Whether you're decades out from retirement or not planning on retiring at all, you can still adjust your current spending so that you have more money to save. In fact, you can make major lifestyle changes that reduce your spending substantially. Consider the changes you'd be willing to make; think about how that added savings might impact your future plans.

Tips for Income Planning

The topic of income planning is one that could be covered in multiple volumes. There are so many different strategies and products out there that could be discussed. Among all the income planning ideas and strategies are some universal rules that everyone should know. These are:

- **Delay taking Social Security:** The longer you wait to start taking Social Security, the higher your monthly payment will be. In fact, if you delay taking it at full retirement age and wait until age 70, you can earn delayed retirement credits that increase your payments even more. Since you hit the maximum payment amount at age 70, there is little point in waiting past that time to start taking benefits. Depending on your date of birth and that of your spouse, there may be other claiming strategies available to you that can substantially increase your lifetime Social Security earnings, which is something I'll discuss in more detail in Chapter 6.

- **Build an income-focused portfolio:** A portfolio built for income takes time, risk tolerance, taxes, and guarantees into consideration. It contains a variety of products such as annuities, bonds, life insurance policies, and CDs. It is also annually rebalanced to ensure that it continues to meet your needs.
- **Limit your withdrawals:** Just because you can start withdrawing money from your savings upon retirement doesn't mean it can become a free-for-all. Look at the performance of your portfolio and, whenever possible, rein in your withdrawals so they don't affect your principal.
- **Consider a reverse mortgage:** Your home's equity could contribute to your lifestyle expenses through a reverse mortgage. This will give you either a lump sum or regular income payments that don't need to be paid back until after you pass away or decide to sell your home.

Avoiding the Traps of Old Planning Wisdom

Old wives' tales, superstitions, and urban legends sometimes stick around in our folklore because they have a kernel of truth in them. This is true of carrots helping your vision and raw garlic helping prevent the common cold, for example. But usually, these myths get recirculated just because we've heard them so often and for so long, we assume they must be true.

Patrick T. Lyman, CAS, CSA, RFC, RHU

This is an especially dangerous assumption when it comes to old financial planning wisdom, because of the constantly changing nature of finance and the economy. Let's look at several retirement planning myths that desperately need to be dropped from our collective consciousness.

- **MYTH: The 4 percent rule.** This myth asserts that as long as you limit yourself to withdrawing no more than 4 percent of your retirement account balance each year, you won't run out of money.
  - **Truth:** Limiting yourself to withdrawals of a certain percentage of your balance makes sense, but the underlying performance of your investments will dictate the percentage limit. With current interest rates, the 4 percent rule is outdated. The newly recommended withdrawal rate is 2.8 percent, according to research completed by economists and financial analysts.[11] Ultimately, your percentage of withdrawal should align with actual investment performance.
- **MYTH: You can always work.** Many people believe they can work continuously through their retirement years and, if they choose to retire but experience financial difficulties, they can always get a part-time job to help them out.

---

[11]https://www.investopedia.com/articles/personal-finance/030613/why-4-rule-no-longer-works-retirees.asp

- - o **Truth:** In 2019 the Employee Benefit Research Institute found that 80 percent of workers said they were expecting to continue to work for pay while in retirement, yet only 28 percent of them actually do.[12]
  - **MYTH: You need to save at least $1,000,000 before you can retire.** How many times have you heard that $1,000,000 is the baseline figure you need to retire comfortably? Probably more than once.
    - o **Truth:** You may need more than $1,000,000, and you may be able to get away with less. It depends on your other sources of postretirement income, your lifestyle expectations, your living expenses, and so much more. A single number can provide a goal to reach for or a starting point for developing your income strategy, but true income planning should take your personal situation, investment performance, and needs into consideration.
  - **MYTH: My kids will take care of me.** You've probably heard statistics stating that as many as 20 million people are taking care of a parent aged 65 or older.[13] But what does that really mean?

---

[12]https://www.investopedia.com/articles/personal-finance/101515/planning-retiring-later-think-again.asp

[13]https://www.pewresearch.org/fact-tank/2015/11/18/5-facts-about-family-caregivers/

- **Truth:** Your kids might be able to take care of you as you age and need help with activities of daily living, such as bathing and dressing, but there are no guarantees that they will be able or willing to. Instead of taxing your relationship with these expectations, getting long-term care insurance will ensure you can get the care you need, without putting any burden on your children. And even if they can help you with some errands and household tasks, that doesn't mean they will help you with your finances. In fact, it's been found that 58 percent of those helping care for an aging parent are helping just with errands, housework, and home repairs.[14] Which means you still need to have an income plan.
- **MYTH: Your expenses will be lower in retirement.** With your children raised and living on their own, your debt paid off, and no need to invest in work clothing or commuting, you should be looking at lower expenses in retirement ... right?
  - **Truth:** Being retired doesn't automatically mean you will have lower expenses. In fact, you could spend more than you did while working. Why? Because instead of spending all your day at work, retirement frees up your time to travel, take classes, indulge in

---

[14] https://www.pewresearch.org/fact-tank/2015/11/18/5-facts-about-family-caregivers/

your hobbies, take midweek trips, and so much more. In addition, you have inflation and rising taxes working against you. Then, there are the increased medical expenses most retirees experience. All in all, it's easy to imagine your spending being the same or even more than it was, at least during the early years of your retirement.

Retired

At this point, you have very little time to recover from mistakes made from believing in popular retirement myths. Rather than putting your faith, and your money, into what you think is a tried-and-true retirement strategy, talk to an advisor you trust and review your retirement plan.

Soon to retire

You can hurt yourself now, before retirement, if your investing and savings strategies follow out-of-touch approaches. Talk to an advisor to see how you can modernize your retirement plan and get the most out of your resources.

Not planning to retire

Always remember that when it comes to planning never to retire, the statistics are not on your side. While it's perfectly understandable to aim for never retiring, at least plan for a potential late retirement, just in case.

Chapter 4 Checklist

__ Complete the postretirement income needs assessment.

__ Consider which of the income planning tips you can incorporate into your plan.

__ Think about some other retirement planning myths you believe and research their accuracy.

The Path to a Stress-Free Retirement

Patrick T. Lyman, CAS, CSA, RFC, RHU

Chapter 5

The Value of Guarantees

In the world of finance, guarantees are few and far between. Your stockbroker will probably never utter the word. Neither will your 401(k) or 403(b) plan administrator or IRA custodian.

A guarantee is different from an expectation or projection. While it's not without risk, the risks are different from those that nonguaranteed products are exposed to. There are some investments, such as corporate bonds, that may have lower risks and fixed returns. Yet even these instruments, which are issued with a promise that your principal will be returned at maturity, don't have a guarantee, since bond issuers can and do default. This means the interest rate, while set at a predetermined, fixed rate, is not entirely guaranteed.

If you go deep enough, you'll find that guarantees in finance do exist. CDs covered under FDIC insurance and municipal bonds are two investments that have some backup, allowing issuers to make guarantees of repayment. Life insurance policies have guaranteed death benefits and some even have guaranteed cash value growth.

Another option for a guaranteed investment is an annuity. Even better, with an annuity there is some greater opportunity for growth if the annuity is structured correctly. Before we get into too much detail about what annuities are, though, let's talk about why the guarantees they offer are so important.

Guarantees versus Fixed Interest

There are a variety of ways for investments to be structured. Generally, returns are either fixed or variable. A variable return would be like that of a stock. It can change at a moment's notice, and there's no preset amount that you've been promised. A bond, on the other hand, can have a fixed coupon or interest rate. This means that the bond is designed to pay out an established rate continually until maturity.

It's important that investors not confuse a fixed interest rate with a guaranteed return. The central difference between the two is:

A fixed rate promises a certain rate will be earned, but does not guarantee that it will be paid out.

Let's look at a bond as an example. If you have a $10,000 corporate bond with a fixed interest rate of 5 percent, it means that you are entitled to periodic interest payments of $500. It does not, however, mean that the bond issuer is guaranteeing you that those payments will be made. In fact, they might default on the bond issue and pay nothing. That's part of the risk you take in exchange for the potential return.

A guarantee is different in that it's a legal promise to make a payment. Usually these guarantees are backed by insurance entities or legal requirements for the issuer to maintain certain cash assets set aside from risk.

When it comes to planning your paycheck for life, fixed interest products are a great addition to your portfolio because they help mitigate the risks of loss introduced by variable products. For example, a 5 percent fixed return on a bond can help reduce the losses you feel when the stock market falls and your stocks lose money.

But these products are not without risks. After all, in the first three quarters of 2019, we saw 85 companies around the world fail to make their bond payments.[15] So while fixed investments are great in theory, further risk reduction is required, and that's often achieved by adding products with guarantees.

Guarantees versus Projections

When you add a volatile, unpredictable investment, such as a stock, mutual fund, or floating-rate bond to your portfolio, you won't get any guarantees about how it will perform. It would be impossible to give you a guarantee because investments like these are subject to the ups and downs of the markets. Essentially, the value of the

---

[15] https://www.barrons.com/articles/more-companies-have-defaulted-in-2019-than-all-of-2018-51570443300

investment at the time you decide to liquidate is the amount you will get for it, and no one can make a guarantee of what that amount will be on those types of investments.

Sometimes, however, when you're evaluating what funds to buy, you will be shown a chart that illustrates the past performance of a specific fund, usually over one, three, five, 10, and 15-year terms. This is called a projection, and it is not a prediction of performance. Let's look at an example.

On the following page is an example of the type of projection you might see in a mutual fund prospectus. It presents an average rate of return for several funds based on different asset classes and mixes. While it's easy to look at the Aggressive mix and see the 10.02 percent average return and assume that means you can count on an annual 10.02 percent return when investing in that fund, it simply isn't the case.

In fact, there could be years when you have a negative return and lose money with this fund, and other years when you earn far less than 10.02 percent. It's also possible that the return is so low for a number of years that it doesn't even keep up with inflation. While that's a risk you may want to take with some of your money, it's not a good option for those who want to create a regular, reliable income out of their savings.

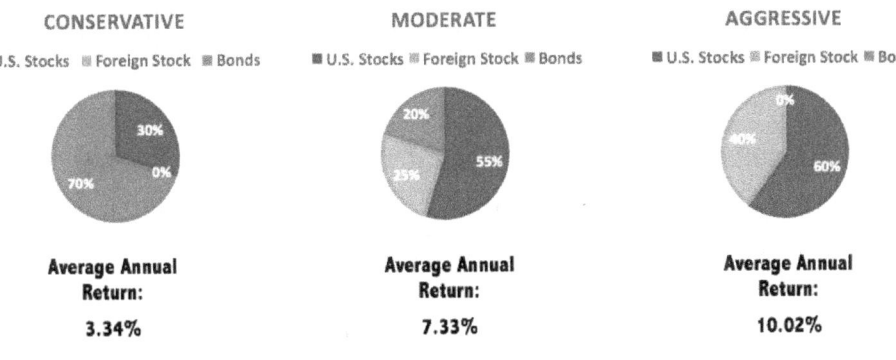

FIGURE 7

SAMPLE ONLY. NOT A GUARANTEE OF PERFORMANCE.

To put it bluntly, a projection is a guess about future value based on past performance. Not exactly something you should gamble your whole retirement on, is it?

Instead, you want to look at putting some portion of your savings into an investment product that offers you a guarantee of future value.

Unlike a projection, which provides you with a hopeful look at the way an investment could potentially perform, a guarantee is a promise of a return. It's a specified, contractual obligation for a set return—not a hope or a guess, but a promise you can count on. When it comes to creating a postretirement income, a guarantee is something you can develop your budget around; a projection is not.

Guarantees and Accumulation: The Secret of an Annuity

Some think that if they buy an investment with a guarantee, it means they are giving up something to get that guarantee. Many assume that they are trading the ability to accumulate returns in exchange for a guarantee. But that's not always the case.

Sometimes, like with a CD paying 1 percent over five years, you are exchanging safety and security for growth, and that can definitely have a place in your portfolio. But with some products such as annuities, you can continue to accumulate capital while ensuring there's no risk of losing your principal.

Let's look at some of the annuity's unique features to get a better understanding.

- **Accumulation:** The process of accumulating assets boils down to proper balance of risk and reward. After all, if you invest in a high-risk investment hoping to accumulate returns, and you lose money that you don't have time to re-earn, then the risk exceeded the value of the potential reward. Annuities help balance potentially substantial rewards with extreme protection—including protection of principal. When you have a fixed indexed annuity, you're participating in the market so you're able to grow your balance as the market climbs. But when the market falls, the built-in safety net ensures that your principal is preserved.

- **Professional management:** For many pre- and postretirees, maintaining a fully managed portfolio isn't practical. Between the cost of the asset management and the minimum account values required, pre- and postretirees often find they either don't qualify for or can't afford that level of attention. That is, unless they get a fixed indexed annuity with a benchmark index. Many of these annuities even have monthly or quarterly rebalancing to ensure the returns are stabilized in a fluctuating market. Even better, they have a floor that prevents losses of principal—something no other managed account will provide.
- **Custom design:** Your life, your income needs, your legacy desires, your asset balance—these are all different from every other retiree's. So why should you try a one-size-fits-all product when you don't have a one-size-fits-all life? Annuities allow for complex design options that can offer survivorship options, death benefits, nursing home benefits, free withdrawals, and so much more.
- **Guaranteed income potential:** When we're saving and accumulating assets for retirement, what are we really doing? Are we trying to amass a limitless amount of cash to try to pay for limitless potential expenses in a completely unpredictable retirement? Or are we trying to ensure that we have enough money to pay ourselves throughout our retirement years, no matter how long those last? If the latter, then why not just cut to the chase and look for

guaranteed income instead of hopeful returns? Not only do annuities guarantee the safety of your principal but they can also be structured with an income payout guarantee. This allows you to take an annual distribution from your annuity of a set amount over your entire lifetime, regardless of how much (or how little) your annuity grew. In fact, the benefit will continue to be paid out even if the contract runs out of money—in other words, even if the payment of your income exceeds your deposited principal.

- **Built-in diversification:** A diversified portfolio is one that has a variety of investments in various industries, markets, sectors, and countries. But annuities go further than that. Not only do the assets within the annuity get rebalanced and diversified over a broad spectrum (based on features and mechanics of a particular market or index), but they also add extra benefits that aren't correlated with a market or any performance indicators at all. These include the guaranteed income rider and death benefits.
- **Principal protection and other risk minimization:** Emotions are often an Achilles' heel when it comes to retirement saving. Fear and greed, two powerful emotions, can lead us to make major investing mistakes—selling out of positions and locking in losses when we get scared of market dips, or investing heavily in risky positions to chase returns are two examples. For many preretirees,

mistakes made by emotional investing can completely undermine their goal of creating a lifetime income with their savings. The built-in diversification, management, and guarantees all serve to protect annuity buyers from risks discussed in past chapters. In addition to those protections, annuities ensure that investors are less likely to react emotionally to market-moving triggers for two major reasons:

- With principal protected from losses and guaranteed income payments, there is far less incentive to react to fear and start selling and less incentive to let greed take over to chase returns.
- Designed for long-term investment, annuities have surrender fees that discourage moving money out early.

There is a little-known reason that accumulation is a dangerous focus for retirement savers: we simply aren't accumulating enough. According to the National Retirement Risks Index, at least 50 percent of working adults in the US are at high risk of not accumulating enough to support their current lifestyle during retirement.[16] Why? A recession in 2008, market dips, poorly performing assets, low bond, savings, and CD rates—the reasons are endless.

Especially at risk for the problems caused by limited accumulation are seniors and those approaching

---

[16]https://crr.bc.edu/special-projects/national-retirement-risk-index/

retirement, because as you age and your working years wind down, you are increasingly advised to move your assets out of high-risk positions (which can create far better accumulation opportunities) into more conservative, lower-risk, lower-reward positions.

This is yet another reason why focusing on guarantees—both for performance and income—is a critical step toward ensuring you have enough to support your retirement lifestyle objectives.

Retired

It's not too late to secure guarantees on your savings, even if you're already retired. You can still look for products that offer guarantees, including guaranteed income, and have them start paying immediately or within a few years.

Soon to retire

Investing in products with guarantees is a great way to help ensure that you get to retire when you want to. With products like annuities offering guaranteed income streams, you can structure the product to pick up right where your current career ends. Then, you can ensure you never have to go without an income.

Under 55 or not planning to retire

Even if you're not planning on retiring, investing in products with guarantees ensures that you put your

> money to work for you in the most efficient way. It also means that you can better preserve your principal for your heirs.

A Closer Look at Fixed Index Annuities

There are a number of different annuity options for people who want to include one in their retirement income plan.

Generally, fixed index annuities offer a good mix of protection, guarantees, and growth, which is why I like to focus on this product. When talking to an advisor about your specific situation, however, you might be directed to a different product. It all depends on what's suitable for you.

There is one major reason that I like to talk about fixed index annuities (FIAs) and why I think they can be a strong contender for postretirement income protection: FIAs offer investors protection against losses and lifetime income guarantees. If you know anything about the stock market, you know that these are outstanding features you won't get with most investments.

But there are even more differences that set FIAs apart from other investments, especially the stock market.

FIAs vs. the Stock Market

One argument you might hear is that you should put your money in the stock market instead of FIAs. While a balanced portfolio includes a mix of different investments, one that's heavily invested in the stock market could be far less efficient and safe than one that includes a fixed index annuity. To better understand why that is, let's look at some of the ways FIAs are different from investments with stock market exposure.

- **The stock market is volatile.** If you retire at age 65 with a Traditional IRA holding $1,000,000 in stocks, you might feel secure, but think about this: Will that $1,000,000 value still be $1,000,000 in a week? A month? A year? The truth is, the very day after you retire, your stock portfolio could lose a tremendous amount of value. Every single moment that the stock market is open, the value of your holdings can and may change—and not always for the better. FIAs don't have the same volatility. In fact, some of them have frequent rebalancing to make sure that volatility is smoothed out, so you don't get seasick watching the ups and downs of your portfolio value.
- **FIAs can come with income guarantees.** Let's think about that $1,000,000 stock portfolio value again. Does it guarantee you a lifetime income? Are there any guarantees you will be able to pull out a certain amount every single year, no matter how long you live or how far the stock market drops? Here's the answer: No, there are no income guarantees. That's something you can only get with a properly designed annuity.
- **Stocks expose you to sequence of return risk.** When you need to pull funds out of your retirement savings to pay for living expenses, food, medications, insurance, and other normal expenses, you can't necessarily wait around for the stock

market to have a good day before you sell stock and take the funds. That means you may have to sell some of your positions when they are down—and if that's the case, you will have to sell more shares than you would if the stocks were up.

For example, if you have 100 shares of XYZ stock and in the days before you need the cash, that stock is priced at $100 per share, you only need to sell 10 shares to get $1,000. You then still have 90 shares growing that you can later sell. If, however, the stock is only worth $60 per share at the time you need the funds, then you would have to sell 17 shares to get that same amount, leaving 83 shares in your portfolio. Selling more shares at a lower value means having fewer shares still invested and growing—and fewer shares available to sell later.

This is an even bigger concern when it happens during the early years of your retirement, which is what many seniors dealt with when they retired in 2008 as the Great Recession was kicking off. This essentially is sequence of return risk. With a fixed index annuity, not only is there an option for a guaranteed lifetime income, you are also removed from sequence of return risk because FIAs put a floor on your performance that protects you against losses.

- **FIAs put a limit on losses.** When you're invested in stocks or, for that matter, mutual funds, corporate bonds, and other variable investments, you are exposed to potential losses. There is always a chance that a stock's price will fall below the price it was when you bought it; that a mutual fund's net asset value will drop; that a bond issuer will default without paying back interest or principal. While you can hedge against these losses, there is no way to invest in those instruments and remove your exposure to loss. FIAs give you access to a large portion of the upside you could get from investing in stocks, but they take away that major downside of potential losses.

- **FIA fees are affordable and cover income guarantees, enhanced death benefits, and other add-on riders.** Just about all investments have some cost associated with owning, buying, and/or selling them. As an example, stocks have commission fees and mutual funds have expense fees and loads. But FIAs have fees that guarantee a higher death benefit payout to your survivors, a guaranteed income for your entire life, and other added benefits. A completely plain, basic FIA with no lifetime income guarantees and a death benefit that simply equals the current net value has no fees, which is also worth considering for your portfolio. When it comes to asset management in the annuity, the cap on the upside and the participation rates allow for there to be no fee for management. In newer annuities with customized indices and rebalancing, a spread might be charged between the gains made and those paid out. It's worth noting

that none of these situations impacts the amount of lifetime income that's paid out on the annuity. Further, asset management and rebalancing of a stock portfolio would require you to pay a percentage of your portfolio value to an asset manager every year.
- **Annuities offer death benefits.** When your assets are tied up in the stock market, the market determines how much your heirs inherit, not you. With an annuity, you can design the contract to have a set death benefit, based either on the investment in the contract or enhanced with a fee-based rider, so you know exactly how much your heirs are guaranteed when you pass away. Some annuities even offer a step-up rider that allows the death benefit to exceed the principal paid for the annuity.

No single product is a perfect fit for everyone. There are some people who may find that a fixed index annuity suits their needs, objectives, and risk tolerance, and there are some who might find that another type of annuity, such as variable, is a better fit.

But generally speaking, fixed index annuities have a variety of features and benefits that make them a solid addition to a portfolio of someone who's working on a long-term income distribution plan.

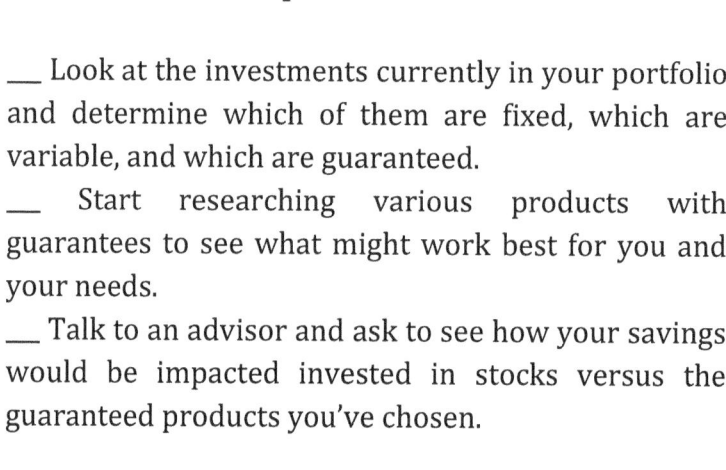

Chapter 5 Checklist

__ Look at the investments currently in your portfolio and determine which of them are fixed, which are variable, and which are guaranteed.

__ Start researching various products with guarantees to see what might work best for you and your needs.

__ Talk to an advisor and ask to see how your savings would be impacted invested in stocks versus the guaranteed products you've chosen.

Patrick T. Lyman, CAS, CSA, RFC, RHU

Chapter 6

Finding the Right Pension and Social Security Elections

Social Security is an important component of any senior's late-in-life income planning, whether they plan to retire or not. You might be tempted to overlook its importance, see it as a "bonus," or even take this payment for granted, but the truth is you need a Social Security strategy so you can maximize what you get. To help explain why, I'm going to share a story with you.

Introducing Clive and Sarah

Now, this story is not based on a specific client. It's more of an amalgam of so many different clients and friends I've had, all of whom I've helped avoid making the same mistake, which is taking Social Security too early.

For Clive and Sarah, our sample couple, the plan was originally to begin taking Social Security at age 62. For Clive, that would have meant taking his first payment in 2020. For Sarah, that would have meant a first payment in 2021.

Clive and Sarah are both in good health, have grown children, and no debt. They are both employed but feel they've accomplished enough professionally to happily retire. If they both retire at age 62, then their combined monthly income from Social Security will be $4,201, or $50,412 per year. On top of this, they plan to take an annual income from their retirement savings, which consists of an IRA and two 401(k) plans.

Every year, Social Security gives seniors a cost-of-living (COLA) adjustment. If we assume a COLA rate of 1.5 percent, which is in line with actual inflation rates, and a life expectancy of 90 years for each of them Clive and Sarah can expect to take in a total of $1,802,937 from Social Security over roughly 28 years. Not bad!

Not bad ... but it could be better. Since Clive and Sarah are healthy and vibrant, have careers they both enjoy, and have no pressing, urgent plans for their retirement, there's no reason they can't explore the idea of waiting longer to retire. But, it needs to be worth it, right? In a scenario that seems as if it's right out of a movie, I could ask Clive and Sarah if they would be willing to work for another eight years to get an extra half-million dollars.

Seriously! If they delay their Social Security to age 70, Clive and Sarah can keep working at careers they enjoy, keep earning an income, keep making contributions to their retirement savings, and expect to get $8,318 per month from Social Security. And with that annual COLA increase estimated at 1.5 percent, they can expect to have received $2,298,422 over 20 years.

You might think this is just an odd, one-off example, but you'd be wrong. Because Clive and Sarah are not unusual. Let's look at another couple, Luke and Ann.

Let's Meet Luke and Ann

Now, Luke and Ann are in a different situation. Their kids are gone, but they have some debt. Luke loves his career and feels like he has a lot to offer his industry, but Ann doesn't feel the same level of career satisfaction as she once did.

Ann, who is 60, really wants to retire at age 62. Luke, who is 62, is considering retiring at 63. If they do this, they will get a respectable $4,905 monthly from Social Security. If Luke lives to age 88 and Ann to age 90, they will have received a total of $1,539,457.

But, and it's important to consider this, because they still have debt, they will lose some of that money to interest payments.

Now Ann really doesn't want to work until age 70— no matter how much higher her Social Security payment would be then. And I understand that. Luke, on the other hand, doesn't seem to mind.

Looking at their total debt, if they stay on budget and Ann works another few years, they can get out of debt by the time Ann is 66. If she were to retire at 66 and Luke were to work until 70, they would almost double their monthly Social Security income, getting $8,596 total.

Better yet, if Ann lives to 90 and Luke to 88, they would see a total of $1,909,874 in benefits.

But what if Luke and Ann, or Clive and Sarah, want to retire earlier? Does that mean they have to give up those higher Social Security payments? Not at all. If they have another plan in place for income distributions after retirement, they can rely on that to pay their living expenses and leave Social Security untouched until later years.

At What Age Should YOU Take Social Security?

You now have a better sense of the importance of creating a Social Security strategy and, as part of that, delaying payments for as long as you can, up until age 70 (at which point delayed retirement credits stop). Even if you can only delay a month or two, it will make a difference.

Look at this chart from the Social Security Administration, showing the change in benefits for those who wait one month or more after reaching full retirement age.

PROVIDED UNDER CREATIVE COMMONS FROM SSA.GOV
How Delayed Retirement Affects Your Social Security Benefits

If you start getting benefits at age*	Multiply your Full Retirement Benefit by
66	100%
66 + 1 month	100.7%
66 + 2 months	101.3%
66 + 3 months	102.0%
66 + 4 months	102.7%
66 + 5 months	103.3%
66 + 6 months	104.0%
66 + 7 months	104.7%
66 + 8 months	105.3%
66 + 9 months	106.0%
66 + 10 months	106.7%
66 + 11 months	107.3%

FIGURE 8

More money isn't the only factor at play when you determine the best age for you to begin taking Social Security. Other factors to consider include:

- **Your health.** If you have health issues that make working difficult or chronic illnesses that could shorten your lifespan, then taking benefits early might be worthwhile.
- **Ability to continue working.** Working takes a toll on us emotionally, physically, and mentally. As you

age, you may find yourself increasingly challenged by these tolls and unable to continue as long as you once thought possible.

- **Your income needs.** As we age, many of our expenses decline. But some, such as medical care, can increase. Even if you continue working, you may find that you have trouble making ends meet and need Social Security to supplement your income.
- **What other income you can rely on.** You may have income to pull from annuities, life insurance policies, pensions, and retirement plans that can help you delay taking Social Security.
- **Your potential tax bracket.** When you continue to work and earn money or draw taxable income from retirement accounts, that income is combined with a percentage of your Social Security income to determine your tax bracket and the amount of Social Security that's taxable. In some cases, it might be better to wait to take Social Security income until your overall income falls, so you can minimize any taxes due on those distributions.

Ultimately, you want to understand what will happen with your Social Security benefits in a variety of scenarios. When working with a financial advisor, you can ask them to look at several situations for you. That way you can see how different choices will turn out and measure whether their impact is worth it.

Breaking Even

One way to decide when to take your benefits is by calculating your break-even point. We know from reading the stories of Clive and Sarah and Luke and Ann that there is a big difference between the overall lifetime amount you might get from Social Security depending on the age when you start taking benefits, and the number of years you collect those benefits. In some cases, taking benefits early can end up paying out more if you have a shorter lifespan.

Finding your break-even point means determining the age at which the amount collected from an early payout matches the amount collected from a later payout. For example, let's assume your full retirement age is 66:

- If you can expect to get $1,500 per month at 66 but can only get $1,150 per month by taking early retirement a month after turning 62, then you will take home a total of $54,050 during the 47 months between turning 62 and turning 66.
- If you wait until age 66 to collect, then over the course of 13 years, you will have taken home the same amount as you would have if you started taking benefits at age 62. That is your break-even point.

So, the question you should ask yourself in this situation is whether you expect yourself to live past the break-even point, which is age 79 in this example. If you do, then you should delay taking Social Security for as long as possible. If not, then taking it early makes sense.

To work this out for yourself, follow these steps:

1. Write down your monthly benefit at full retirement.
2. Use the calculators at SSA.gov to determine your benefit if you start taking payments at an earlier age. The calculator will need information like your Social Security number, date of birth, and mother's maiden name.
3. Multiply the amount of your early benefit by the number of months before you reach full retirement age.
4. Subtract your early payment and your full retirement age payment. Take the total you got for step 3 and divide that by the result, which is the difference between those two payments.
5. The number you get is the number of months it would take you to break even after starting early distributions.

Pension Options

Another consideration you'll need to make when you retire with a pension is whether to take a life-only payout of benefits or a joint-life payout.

With a life-only payout, the pension benefits cease upon the death of the pension holder. With a joint-life payout, benefits continue being paid after death to the surviving spouse. If you aren't married, then the choice will be easy. If you are married, you need to review the difference between the payout amounts and evaluate whether it makes more sense to take a larger payout over a single-life or maintain benefits after the pension holder passes away.

Some of the factors that will weigh into the decision include:

- Amount of savings
- Whether the single-life benefits are large enough to keep you from tapping into other savings
- What each of the spouse's individual Social Security and pension benefits are
- Health and life expectancy of each spouse
- Total taxable income at retirement, i.e., tax bracket at retirement

---

Retired

If you've already retired and/or started taking Social Security benefits, it's still worth doing the break-even calculation, as long as you started benefits fewer than 13 months ago. If you have, and your breakeven makes you wish you'd delayed benefits, you may be able to pay back the benefits received so far and withdraw your claim.[17] Then, you can restart benefits at a later date. But remember, this is only allowable in the first 12 months you receive benefits.

Soon to retire

This is a great time to figure out your Social Security break-even point. And while that will play a part in your decision on when to start taking payments,

---

[17] https://www.ssa.gov/planners/retire/withdrawal.html

remember that financial need also plays a role.

Under 55 or not planning to retire

Even if you don't plan to ever retire, you still need to figure out the best time to take your Social Security benefits. After all, you are entitled to the benefits and they do not get passed on to family members if you don't take them.

Chapter 6 Checklist

__ Ask an advisor to show you the different Social Security payout options facing you so you get a handle on your potential lifetime payout based on different retirement ages.

__ Figure out your break-even point.

__ Review your pension payout options and, if you're married, discuss with your spouse the best options for you both.

Patrick T. Lyman, CAS, CSA, RFC, RHU

Chapter 7

Inheritance and Income Planning

Whether through unspent savings, stock portfolios, life insurance, annuities, real property, or antiques, an inheritance is something that many people will receive as they head into retirement. Does that mean you should count on it being your means of paying for retirement? Not if you're smart.

The Reality of Inheritance

To understand what inheritances look like these days, I want you to see some research findings from a few different sources. This should clue you in on how wide the gulf is between our expectations and reality. First, the expectations:

- According to an HSBC survey, 27 percent of respondents who have received or expect to receive an inheritance assume that the inheritance will either largely or totally fund their retirement.[18]
- The same survey found that 66 percent think they will receive an inheritance that will at least *help* fund their retirement.

So far, so good, right? But now let's look at the reality of inheritances:

- Research conducted by the Federal Reserve in 2013 found that the wealthiest 5 percent of households in the US had an average inheritance of $1.1 million. The average for the middle 45 percent was $183,000, and the average for the bottom 50 percent was just $68,000—not exactly retirement-fund-building amounts.[19]

Of course, a five- or six-figure inheritance could help fund a retirement and might even last five or more years, right? Maybe not ...

- One-third of inheritance recipients studied in 2015 had negative savings just two years after receiving their inheritance.[20]

---

[18] http://www.hsbc.com/news-and-insight/insight-archive/2015/the-issue-of-leaving-a-legacy
[19] Federal Reserve, "Survey of Consumer Finances," Oct. 24, 2014
[20] https://www.marketwatch.com/story/one-in-three-americans-

And now, just to stress the point that you cannot bank on an inheritance:

- An HSBC survey across 15 countries found a full 21 percent of recipients thought their heirs should earn their own wealth, with no inheritance from relatives.[21]

The truth is, not only do you not know IF you will get an inheritance, you also don't know when you might get one and how much it will be. That's why an inheritance should be used to supplement retirement savings, rather than being counted on to create it.

In my book, *Your 30-Day Retirement Plan*, I have an exercise where you can create three different postretirement budgets for yourself. One is based on a financial crisis, one is based on your ideal lifestyle, and one is based on a reduction from your ideal. An inheritance, if and when you get one, can be used to bump up your overall postretirement budget.

If you're in financial crisis mode before the inheritance, it may help you add another few hundred dollars a month and possibly reach your lesser ideal. If you're living at your lesser ideal, an inheritance might help

---

who-get-an-inheritance-blow-it-2015-09-03

[21] http://www.hsbc.com/news-and-insight/insight-archive/2015/the-issue-of-leaving-a-legacy

you add a few thousand a year and get closer to your ideal lifestyle.

But all your planning should be based on what you _KNOW_ you have, which would be your savings, assets, and investments.

The Emotional Dynamics of Inheritance

Once you understand how to gain proper perspective on the idea of an inheritance in terms of where it fits in your financial life, you next must consider how the emotional impact will affect you.

Recently, a married couple who I've worked with were surprised to find out that the wife's mother had left them a substantial inheritance. The two had expected a small inheritance but had no idea they would end up with seven figures, thanks to the annuity and life insurance planning the mother had done.

Since the mother had never spoken to them about the estate and did not prepare them for what to expect, they were completely broadsided when they started getting bombarded with letters from insurance companies and then received a summary from the estate executor.

What surprised them both about this, besides the sheer amount of money involved, was the emotional impact of the large inheritance. The amount of their inheritance changed their lives completely overnight, a dream come true—in theory. But when that life change is celebrated at the expense of losing a loved one, there is a tremendous amount of guilt attached.

In addition, suddenly being a millionaire—or even having six figures handed to you after struggling to get by—can be overwhelming. While my clients got the same inheritance as the other siblings, that isn't always the case. Which adds another dimension of guilt, confusion, and maybe even resentment.

All this emotional turmoil can, unfortunately, lead to some reluctance or hesitance when it comes to planning ways to optimize the inheritance and incorporate it into a distribution plan. As emotionally complex, raw, and overwhelming as it is, the best thing you can do to honor the person who left the inheritance is to make sure you properly plan so you can ensure those funds have a positive impact on your life and on the lives of those you will leave behind.

Honor the giver by making sure the legacy you've been entrusted with is wisely used and possibly even passed on through multiple generations.

The Practicalities

Gaining an inheritance doesn't mean that money falls into your lap and your only job is to figure out how to spend it. I could fill an entire book with the process of claiming your inheritance, but here I want to focus on those aspects that impact your retirement distribution plan.

Requesting Funds

Once you learn that there's an inheritance waiting for you, you have to go through the steps of claiming it. To start, you'll need several copies of the death certificate. You'll also need a way to track the different types of investments, companies, account numbers, and other information for the sources of your inherited funds.

Once you're ready to start requesting the funds, you'll want to keep track of the process. I suggest creating a spreadsheet with the following 13 columns (explanation has been added where necessary):

Investment/account type: Your inheritance may come through a bank account balance, an annuity, a life insurance policy, a mutual fund, an IRA, or any number of other vehicles. Since each one will have its own terms, conditions, rules, withdrawal requirements and tax status, it's important to keep track of this.

- Company/institution name
- Account number
- Original owner: The deceased isn't always the owner of an insurance policy or other account that you are beneficiary of. Make note of the owner in case you need additional information from them or if you need additional information to help the company locate the account when you call.
- Account manager contact info: You may find that you spend a lot of time on the phone when you're trying to get your inheritance. Rather than having to re-explain your situation every time you call a company (something that can be incredibly emotional and taxing), try getting the name and direct number for an account manager who can help you when you call.

- Other beneficiaries: As you process forms, you may discover information that the other beneficiaries need to know. To make this process easier and to get in touch with them over any decisions that must be made together, make sure to track who shares beneficiary status on accounts and investments you are inheriting.
- Taxes taken/planned: Some of the accounts and investments you inherited may be taxable. You might be able to arrange for taxes to be withheld from the distribution amount. If you don't, then you need to plan for them by setting aside the funds. Either way, you need to be prepared for a bill come tax time.
- Paperwork received from company: Every company will have its own set of paperwork to complete to process the claim. When it's a large estate with many different accounts and investments, it's a good idea to track your receipt of the paperwork so you can easily see which companies are lagging on sending it out and contact them.
- Date paperwork submitted: When you start receiving paperwork for a death benefit and inheritance claim, you'll find that sometimes the paperwork is extensive with as many as 12 pages. Other times, it's short. You may have to send back all the pages, or you may only have to complete and send back specified pages. You may also be required to send in supplemental forms, like a copy of the death certificate. Companies don't always

provide a lot of guidance when they send the forms out, so use the contact information you've collected to call and get help with questions. When you send the forms, send them to the right area, using any enclosed envelopes included. Also, make a note of the date so you can call and follow up on progress if it seems to be taking too long.

- Account/method used for deposit: You have many different options for the ultimate deposit of inherited funds, and that can make it hard to keep track of your receipt of funds. For example, you might have an inherited IRA balance rolled over to your own IRA, a life insurance death benefit direct deposited into your savings account, a stock portfolio transferred to a trust, and a mutual fund balance sent to you via check. For each inherited account, policy, and investment, track the account you've instructed the company to pay the benefit to.

- Amount expected: No one is perfect, and that includes insurance companies. Keep track of the amounts you expect to receive and balance what you actually receive against that. And remember, the process of getting your inheritance can take a long time. So don't plan to live on those funds until they are in hand.

- Amount received: This will help you see if there are any discrepancies between the amount you expected and what you got. Remember that if you have taxes withheld, have to liquidate market

assets, or are paying out certain expenses from the proceeds, your final received amount can vary.
- Payments out: Depending on how the estate is handled and/or set up and how many other heirs there are, you may be required to send certain payments out of the proceeds you inherit. These expenses include (but are not limited to):
    - Funeral costs
    - Burial/cremation expenses
    - State and/or federal taxes
    - Inheritance taxes
    - Trustee fees
    - Probate costs
    - Unpaid debts and medical bills
    - Buying out other family member interests in certain assets

What to Do with an Inheritance

Every situation is unique, so it's impossible to give broad advice about what you should do when you receive your inheritance. Often, however, I have found for my clients that simply blending it with their personal assets and making the new funds part of the overall retirement income plan is the best course of action. That may mean purchasing additional fixed index annuities with income guarantees, laddering more CDs, looking at bond and mutual funds, buying additional life insurance, and more.

Of course, there's more to it than that. Other uses for the funds may include:

- Making a charitable gift: There are myriad ways to gift money to a cause, organization, school, or group that you care about. As I'll discuss in the next section, some even allow you to create an income for yourself in retirement through a charitable remainder trust!
- Giving a financial gift to an immediate family member: Advancing part or all of an inheritance to a family member during your lifetime can be a great way to see them celebrate your life and legacy. Just remember that the gift-giver is required to pay gift taxes on all gifts that exceed current IRS limits. In 2019 the annual exclusion for gifts was $15,000 and the lifetime exclusion was $11.4 million.[22]
- Home improvement: From a much-needed roof to updated windows to an extra bathroom, there are many ways that an inheritance can be used to improve an heir's home. To make your inheritance go a step further, consider doing home improvements that:
    - Save money in taxes through energy-efficient upgrades.
    - Add resale value to the property.
    - Ready your home for retirement with safety additions like bars in the bathroom, nonslip floor surfaces, SMART/tech home upgrades, and more.

---

[22]https://www.irs.gov/businesses/small-businesses-self-employed/whats-new-estate-and-gift-tax

- Bucket-list vacation: A once-in-a-lifetime vacation that allows you to check off a line item on your bucket list can be a great way to spend some of your inheritance. Just make sure you have your basic retirement income plan secured before doing so.
- Summer home: Not only can the purchase of a summer home be great fun for you, it can also serve as a family gathering spot that preserves some of your most treasured memories for decades to come.

From Inheritance to Income

In the last section, I briefly mentioned integrating your inheritance into your existing retirement income plan. Now, I want to get into more specifics about this strategy.

An inheritance is a significant gift in itself, but imagine how much more meaningful it can be if you parlay that into a lifetime income that carries you through retirement. No matter how much or how little you inherit, you can do that—you just have to pick the right strategy. Some to consider include:

- Charitable remainder trust: When you add a charitable remainder trust to your legacy plan, you essentially draw a temporary income from an annuity against assets that are gifted to the trust after a specified time. Better yet, you get a partial tax deduction for the donation while you're still living.
- Life insurance: Using your inheritance to fully fund a life insurance policy over a short period of time,

such as five or 10 years, can create a cash value fund that you can access without taxation.
- Dividend stocks: Dividend stocks that regularly pay out a dividend based on the company's earnings. This does make the amount variable, however, so it's a good idea to make this a part of a larger income strategy. If individual stocks aren't your thing, you can also look for dividend funds.
- Bonds: Bonds have coupon rates that promise ongoing, regular interest payments to investors until bond maturity. While this can work to create an income, remember that bond issuers can and do default, so be selective when choosing what bonds you buy. In addition, once a bond matures, you may find that you can't reinvest the principal into a new bond at the same rate, and instead have to choose a lower rate. If your income depends on this interest payment, be sure to adjust your lifestyle expenses accordingly.
- Annuities: As discussed in more detail in Chapter 5, an annuity with an income guarantee can pay out a lifetime income. These annuities can be purchased in a lump sum or in multiple payments.

Another way that an inheritance can help you create a lifetime income is by using it to delay your Social Security. The longer you delay your Social Security (up to age 70), the larger your monthly benefit. If you have an inheritance, especially one that came through a tax-free source like a life insurance death benefit, you can consider relying on that to pay expenses so you don't have to take Social Security until you reach full retirement age—or later!

Talking about Inheritance

One of the most frustrating, yet understandable, aspects of dealing with an inheritance is the unknown. The clients that I mentioned earlier were completely surprised by the amount of their inheritance. That may sound like a good thing, but trying to process that income and determine the most strategic way to handle it, and dealing with insurers and mutual fund companies all while grieving the loss of a mother was a lot for them to handle.

I've also seen the opposite happen; I've had clients who expected a large inheritance without realizing that their loved one had spent the money, had allowed life insurance policies to lapse, or had accumulated massive debt before they died.

These situations are difficult in different ways, but no matter what, they make lives harder—not better.

That's why I advise my clients to be open and honest with their loved ones about their inheritance—or lack thereof. No, that doesn't mean they have to hand over bank statements or report to their children when making a large purchase that could impact their inheritance. It simply means updating your children each year on the types of accounts and investments they will need to deal with, the range of funds they might expect, and helping them create reasonable expectations around how much (or little) they can expect to inherit.

> **Retired**
> It's never too late to consider legacy planning. Even if you think you're limited to the assets you have left as your only legacy, consider ways you might be able to increase that legacy, including through securing life insurance. Many companies continue to issue policies through age 80, and even if you are in ill health, a modified policy with some added accidental death benefits might be possible.

> **Soon to retire**
> At this stage, it can be difficult to manage both retirement planning AND legacy planning. One simple way to do both is to invest in a life insurance policy. Not only will it be less expensive at this age than it would be once you retire but it also means having a fixed monthly premium to pay for your guaranteed legacy amount. The fixed premium will be easier to work into your monthly budget and prevents you from underspending as a means to preserve assets for your heirs.

> **Under 55 or not planning to retire**
> If you aren't planning to retire, or are currently in your 20s or 30s, you may think you can avoid legacy planning. But remember, no matter what plans we have, anything can happen, so it's best to be prepared

for the worst. Create a legacy plan that lays out your objectives for your assets and that ensures your financial priorities are followed well after you're gone.

Chapter 7 Checklist

___ Talk to your parents or other relatives who might be leaving something behind for you and try to get a handle on what to expect.

___ Talk to your children or other heirs about how to handle your estate and what they should expect.

The Path to a Stress-Free Retirement

Patrick T. Lyman, CAS, CSA, RFC, RHU

Chapter 8

Your Paycheck for Life: Customizing Your Income Plan

At this point, you hopefully understand why you should add an income component to your retirement plan and you understand some of the ways you can do that. Now it's time to start the process of figuring out how your plan might look.

This will depend on many different factors, including your personal income needs, your risk tolerance, your priorities, your planned retirement age, and so much more. A full plan should be developed with the help of your financial advisor, but to get started or even to create a mini-plan, you can begin with the following self-assessment.

Self-Assessment

To set up your ultimate retirement income distribution plan, you must ask yourself some tough questions. It's important that you be honest with yourself and that you face the truth of your answers without being defensive, embarrassed, or threatened. After all, the goal is to create a plan that really works for you, and that can only be done when you are willing to be honest, open, and vulnerable.

Retirement income planning is a process of planning for an unpredictable future using the reality of your current financial situation. So, while we have to deal with future hypotheticals, we want to do so using a very tangible current situation.

A professional advisor is the ultimate tool to use when creating your income plan, but you can get started and narrow down some of your choices by asking yourself the following questions:

- Can you handle income distribution on your own? In other words, can you trust yourself to regularly distribute a livable income from your savings and not splurge?
- Are you concerned about your savings lasting a lifetime?
- Is there any point between age 62 and 70 when your Social Security payout alone will be enough to support you?
- When is the latest you think you can practically take Social Security? Consider your health, enthusiasm for your job, and potential tax fallout.

- What is your maximum Social Security payout at age 70? Is it worth finding a way to push back the date you take distributions?
- Based on your anticipated living expenses, what percentage of your current annual income will you need to receive during retirement?
- What percentage of your assets (based on current values) will you need to withdraw to get that amount of income?
- What percentage of your total portfolio is exposed to risks of loss?
- What percentage of your total portfolio do you want exposed to risks of loss when you retire?
- What percentage (if any) of your assets have guarantees? What percentage have complete protection over principal?
- How important is a guarantee of lifetime income regardless of asset performance?
- How tax efficient is your investment plan?
- If you don't have any guaranteed income outside of Social Security, what's your plan for avoiding overspending of your assets?
- How much postretirement income can you expect from the following sources:
    - CD interest
    - Bond interest
    - Dividends
    - Alimony
    - Royalties
    - Rental income and other passive income

- K1 income from business ownership
- At what age do you plan to retire? How many years from now is that? Based on your life expectancy, how many years will that mean you spend in retirement?
- How will required minimum distributions (RMDs) impact your taxes? Whether you like it or not, you'll be forced to start taking distributions from some retirement accounts once you reach age 72 (as of 2020). The amount is based on a uniform table and the balance of your account at the end of the prior year.
- What are your legacy needs?
- Do you already have some legacy planning done, such as an in-force life insurance policy?
- Are you getting the most life insurance benefits for your premium? Could you find a less expensive policy, one with fewer premium payments or more living benefits, such as terminal illness payouts?
- If you had a life insurance policy accruing cash values, could you use the tax-free withdrawals for any postretirement expenses or taxes?
- Does your legacy planning encompass all the charities, people, and causes you care about?
- Is your legacy planning separate from your postretirement income planning so that you don't have to restrict spending to fulfill it?

Putting It All Together

Let's put together everything we've talked about so far by looking at some examples. First up—Clive and Sarah.

Let's assume that Clive and Sarah didn't like the idea of waiting until age 70 to retire, or that maybe they couldn't due to medical issues. So the idea of maximizing Social Security is out the window—or is it?

Not necessarily. If they had $500,000 to put in a fixed indexed annuity, and that annuity paid a premium bonus of 7 percent, they could begin taking withdrawals from that annuity at age 62, totaling $27,050 per year—for life. They could then use those funds to pay their expenses for a few years and push back the date they start Social Security payments.

With that annuity, they would not only have a lifetime annual income but also principal protection and participation in market upswings. And as you can see from the chart on the following page, if they are able to wait before taking distributions from their annuity, they can increase the amount of their guaranteed, lifetime annual income as well.

SAMPLE ONLY. NOT A GUARANTEE OF PERFORMANCE.

Contract Year	Age	Premiums	Bonus	Lifetime Income Benefit Payout
1	61	$500,000.00	$35,000.00	Ineligible
2	62	$0.00	$0.00	$27,050.67
3	63	$0.00	$0.00	$29,334.95
4	64	$0.00	$0.00	$31,795.96
5	65	$0.00	$0.00	$34,446.68
6	66	$0.00	$0.00	$37,229.44
7	67	$0.00	$0.00	$40,222.11
8	68	$0.00	$0.00	$43,439.88
9	69	$0.00	$0.00	$46,898.98
10	70	$0.00	$0.00	$50,616.79
11	71	$0.00	$0.00	$54,516.09
12	72	$0.00	$0.00	$57,039.73
13	73	$0.00	$0.00	$59,665.73
14	74	$0.00	$0.00	$62,397.96
15	75	$0.00	$0.00	$65,240.41
16	76	$0.00	$0.00	$68,086.19

FIGURE 9

And how about Luke and Ann? Luke may be happy working until age 70, but Ann definitely is not. If they found an annuity with a 10 percent bonus and paid a premium of $500,000, they could begin taking guaranteed lifetime annual distributions of $55,680 once Ann reaches age 64. At age 62, she could retire, begin taking her distributions from Social Security while Luke continued to work, and then as Luke starts to wind down his career, she can bump up that income with the annuity—all before Luke has even touched his Social Security.

If Ann waits even longer to take income from her annuity, as you can see from the chart on the following page, she'll increase her guaranteed lifetime annual income even more.

SAMPLE ONLY. NOT A GUARANTEE OF PERFORMANCE.

Contract Year	Age	Premiums	Bonus	Lifetime Income Benefit Payout
1	61	$500,000.00	$50,000.00	Ineligible
2	62	$0.00	$0.00	$24,778.00
3	63	$0.00	$0.00	$26,264.00
4	64	$0.00	$0.00	$27,840.00
5	65	$0.00	$0.00	$32,982.00
6	66	$0.00	$0.00	$34,961.00
7	67	$0.00	$0.00	$37,059.00
8	68	$0.00	$0.00	$39,282.00
9	69	$0.00	$0.00	$41,639.00
10	70	$0.00	$0.00	$48,784.00
11	71	$0.00	$0.00	$51,711.00
12	72	$0.00	$0.00	$51,711.00
13	73	$0.00	$0.00	$51,711.00
14	74	$0.00	$0.00	$51,711.00
15	75	$0.00	$0.00	$56,636.00
16	76	$0.00	$0.00	$56,636.00
17	77	$0.00	$0.00	$56,636.00
18	78	$0.00	$0.00	$56,636.00
19	79	$0.00	$0.00	$56,636.00
20	80	$0.00	$0.00	$61,560.00
21	81	$0.00	$0.00	$61,560.00
22	82	$0.00	$0.00	$61,560.00
23	83	$0.00	$0.00	$61,560.00
24	84	$0.00	$0.00	$61,560.00

FIGURE 10

Retired

If you've already retired, you can still review the questions in the assessment at the beginning of the chapter. Answering them may show you some ways you can change how you're currently spending in retirement, and this might make a significant difference in how long your savings last.

Soon to retire

Right now, you are in the perfect position to start planning and adjusting your spending to help create a lasting retirement income plan.

> **Under 55 or not planning to retire**
> Between delayed retirement credits drying up at age 70 and required minimum distributions (RMDs) starting at age age 72 (as of 2020), you still have some planning to do, even if it's not to support your retirement.

Jon and Hope

Next, let's look at a new couple, Hope and Jon. They're a married couple in their sixties who I met at a retirement seminar during the winter of 2018. They wanted to be able to retire in fall of 2019. At that time, all their assets were in 403(b)s with their current employers. Their goals, in addition to retiring in a year, were to maintain their current lifestyle, leave a legacy for their two children, reduce their risk going forward, create a lifetime income from their current assets, and maintain liquidity levels for emergencies during retirement.

One of their biggest concerns was that they did not want to expose any of Jon's assets to risk after he had retired. At that time, he had a total of almost $500,000 in his 403(b), and he wanted guaranteed income with growth potential and safety of principal.

We recommended a fixed indexed annuity with a very well-known carrier. We structured the annuity to provide them with a substantial monthly withdrawal totaling more than $25,000 per year—for life. This income, combined with their Social Security at full retirement age, was exactly what they needed to maintain their current lifestyle and retire in a single year. It also left some assets in 403(b)s, which they could then access during an emergency. By September 2019, they had started their income plan and retired!

We also did a review of their current life insurance plan. We found that by replacing it, we could save them a significant amount in annual premiums, even reducing the total premium period while also giving them a larger death benefit. Even better, the insurance policy we chose gave them access to cash values so they could start taking tax-free withdrawals after the limited premium period. These withdrawals will help supplement their income going forward.

Peter and Laura

When it comes to savings and accumulation, clients Peter and Laura did great. When they came to see us, they had over $3 million in a brokerage account plus CDs, cash, and other assets. Laura, who is 66, and Peter, who is 69, wanted to maintain their current lifestyle over their full retirement. They also wanted to preserve a small portion of their assets from risk while maintaining liquidity through their lives so they could easily handle the unexpected. Finally, they wanted to have high returns with low risk to principal and to maximize their Social Security.

To help them, we were able to do a nontaxable transfer of cash value from Laura's life insurance policies into a policy that saved them about $17,000 per year in premiums. Even better, the policy had more benefits than the prior policy. It included living benefits such as chronic and terminal illness payments.

To help them maximize Social Security and delay taking distributions, we suggested they move $600,000 from one of their IRAs into an annuity paying a bonus and a guaranteed income to help them avoid taking Social Security. Finally, we moved $500,000 from Peter's IRA into a fixed indexed annuity that matures in just five years and can be surrendered anytime, thus ensuring liquidity while still protecting principal.

Kate and Andrew

Finally, let's look at two more clients, Kate and Andrew. They are a married couple, both aged 66. They wanted to retire but when they saw how much their Social Security payments could be if they waited, they decided they needed to find an alternative to get an income without triggering Social Security.

We found that rolling over Kate's 403(b) and some of her pension benefits into a fixed indexed annuity would help start a guaranteed lifetime income that replaced Social Security and saved about $10,000 in taxes while also gaining a 12 percent bonus on the annuity.

We then had Andrew take his 401(k) balance and roll it into an annuity offering both aggressive accumulation opportunities and a significant death benefit. They each had a Roth IRA, which we left alone. The assets in those IRAs were invested in a variety of instruments, including stocks and mutual funds. This gave them some aggressive upside potential, an acceptable amount of risk exposure, and access to funds that could be liquidated quickly.

Not only are Kate and Andrew's annuity income streams guaranteed for life, but they also will contribute to an increased Social Security payout since they help the couple delay taking payments, they save money in overall fees, they lower risk of principal loss, and they are RMD friendly, so they can meet RMD requirements at age 72 (as of 2020) without charges.

In these cases, we had no need to worry about dividend stocks, bonds, and other vehicles as part of the income plan. Instead, we generally concentrated on allowing investments to serve their purpose as easily liquidated emergency funds. Further, we reduced their overall risk of loss and focused on creating a guaranteed income for life through managing Social Security distributions and selecting guaranteed annuities with bonuses and generous payout guarantees.

We preserved some assets in the market for quick liquidity to deal with emergencies or even large bucket-list expenses. Finally, we preserved legacy planning through life insurance policies so that their income planning wasn't impacted.

These are the solutions that worked best in these situations. There are so many ways to address postretirement income planning, however. These are not the only solutions. To help your advisor better structure your plan to your needs, expectations, and assets, work through the assessment at the beginning of this chapter before your appointment. This will give you a firmer handle on current and anticipated expenses, expectations, needs, concerns, and so on.

One of the most critical aspects of postretirement income planning is assessing risk tolerance and balancing it with rewards. When you rely too heavily on accumulation to fund your retirement, you can easily sink your assets too heavily into risky positions as you're seduced by the opportunity for massive returns. The goal of your assets at retirement is not to add up to a high number, but to support the lifestyle you want to have once you end work.

That is not accomplished through accumulation but through a secure income plan that includes guarantees and principal preservation. Try to get a handle on your risk tolerance by considering how you would feel if you lost your principal versus how you feel about losing an opportunity for high growth. Sorting out those feelings will help you better understand how you tolerate risk and what your overall investing priorities should be.

Retired

If you're looking for the kind of income guarantees and principal protection offered by annuities and you're already retired, you can consider both immediate annuities and life insurance policies to fit your requirements.

Soon to retire

In most of our client stories, we talked about people who were just a few years away from retirement. That means you're in an ideal space to start working with an advisor on isolating the ideal income plan.

Under 55 or not planning to retire

Because annuity income guarantees often allow for increasing distributions the longer you wait to take them, those who don't plan to retire can look at them as long-term disability plans. This way, you can trigger payments should you become disabled.

Chapter 8 Checklist

__ Complete the assessment at the beginning of the chapter.

__ Bring your answers to your next meeting with an advisor.

__ Ask yourself which is worse for you: losing your principal or missing out on growth opportunities.

Patrick T. Lyman, CAS, CSA, RFC, RHU

Chapter 9

Carving Out Your Legacy and Estate Planning

At the beginning of the book, we talked about shifting from distribution to income mindset, and that's what this book has focused on. But right now, I want to revisit distribution because it's a concept that's still relevant in your plan, at least when it comes to your legacy being distributed when you pass away.

Yes, that's right—you can still have assets left to leave to your heirs even after creating a paycheck for life. Paying yourself a dependable income is a vital part of retirement planning, but it doesn't mean that you have to use *all* the assets you've accumulated over the years. In fact, you can build an income plan *and* create an estate for your heirs, which will help them and their future income planning.

You can create a substantial inheritance/estate if you make that a part of your income and distribution planning. Which means you can secure a lifetime income for yourself while also leaving funds behind for your children, your grandchildren, your spouse, your alma mater, your favorite charity, and so much more.

Let's look at three tools that will help you do that.

Life Insurance

Life insurance is one of the simplest, most affordable ways to create a substantial legacy that lasts generations. Like many people, you might think this occurs simply through your death benefit going to your heirs as named beneficiaries. But there's more to it than that.

First, life insurance policies accrue something called "cash values." These are essentially overpaid premiums that you can use as a tax-free fund for big-ticket purchases after retirement. This can keep you from using credit and paying interest after retirement, which will help you preserve some of your assets.

Life insurance policies also have added benefits, called riders, that can give you access to funds to use for nursing home care, terminal illness benefits, and more.

Another legacy-preserving benefit of a life insurance policy is that you can name your favorite nonprofit, school, or organization as the beneficiary of a policy. This greatly expands the footprint of your legacy without impacting the assets you leave behind for family. Alternatively, you can name a funeral home as a full or partial beneficiary of a life insurance policy's proceeds so that your final expenses are completely paid for and, in some cases, so that expenses are locked in and don't have to be paid for by the estate.

Another feature worth mentioning is that life insurance proceeds can also be used to pay taxes, to pay debts against your estate, and to prevent the liquidation of your other assets and real estate when their values are low.

You can gain all these benefits through a single life insurance policy with a range of beneficiaries, by multiple policies, or by appointing a trust as beneficiary of your policy. Through the trust, you can specify how the funds should be spent, split, and distributed as well as when.

Life insurance policies get more expensive as you age, so it's important to secure them as young as possible. In some cases, you may even want to get a mix of permanent and term policies as an affordable way of creating a legacy that decreases in value. This can be especially helpful when you're young and you want to make sure your spouse has enough death benefit to maintain their lifestyle and comfortably raise your children. You can time your policies and their termination so that it corresponds with when your kids are likely to be out on their own and your debt is likely to be paid off.

Annuities

When it comes to legacy planning, life insurance is usually at the top of the list of must-haves. As for annuities? Well, many people believe that these don't have a place in your legacy plan. But they do—and a really important one.

First, we can't ignore the fact that annuities provide many benefits that can help you manage spending and preserve more of your savings for legacy planning. For example, an annuity may provide guaranteed income that keeps you from liquidating stock portfolios. It can also provide nursing home benefits that keep you from spending savings on expensive home health care.

But there are even more reasons to have annuities in your legacy plan, like the fact that they include death benefits and can preserve assets for a charity while still paying you an income.

Annuity death benefits: Annuity death benefits can be structured to pay out to your beneficiaries even after you've begun taking income from the annuity. Some annuities have an option to "step-up" or enhance the death benefit so that it exceeds the principal you paid for the annuity. And this can all be done without requiring any health underwriting for approval.

Charitable remainder trusts: As discussed in Chapter 7, a charitable remainder trust allows you to draw a temporary income from an annuity against assets that are gifted to the trust after a specified period. And, you get a partial tax deduction for the donation while you're still living.

Investments

The investments you accumulate during life, including real estate, vehicles, cash, stocks, antiques, jewelry, and furniture, can all be left behind to benefit your heirs. Because these types of assets don't have named beneficiaries, like a life insurance policy or annuity would, it's vital that you have a detailed will and trust to establish the process of dividing and distributing these assets after your death.

One interesting point about investments and your legacy is that leaving an investment portfolio behind can create a positive tax benefit for your heirs. Taxes must be paid on the gains made in an investment portfolio. So, for example, if you buy 100 shares of XYZ for $400 and sell them later for $500, you will be expected to pay taxes on that $100 gain. This is referred to as a capital gains tax.

Generally, the capital gains tax paid on the sale of investments such as stocks or real estate is based on the difference between the cost of the investment (the basis) and the sale price. This amount is considered your profit, and it establishes your tax liability.

When you pass away and leave these investments to your heirs, however, some of them might be subject to what's called a "step-up" in basis. This means the cost basis is reset to the investment's value on the day you pass away, unless that happens to be lower than your original cost basis. In the case of a mutual fund, the cost basis would be the net asset value at market close on the day assets are transferred to them.

Example: If you buy 100 shares of XYZ for $10 a share and 40 years later, you sell it for $100 a share, your basis is just $1,000, and your gain or profit that you need to pay taxes on is $9,000. If, on the other hand, you buy 100 shares of XYZ for $10 a share and 40 years later, on the day you pass away, it has a market value of $100 a share, the basis could be increased to $10,000 for your heirs. They could then sell it and pay no taxes unless there are estate taxes due.

To find out more about taxes on inherited assets and stepped-up basis, you can visit the IRS website. https://www.irs.gov/pub/irs-utl/21_-_inherited_assets_-_stepped-up_basis.pdf

Legacy planning is an intricate process. With the right guidance and products, you can make sure that all the people and causes you care about are provided for in your legacy, without minimizing your own income.

But legacy planning isn't just about buying products to help you provide a benefit to loved ones and others when you die. It's about ensuring you are well taken care of during your retirement years, that you have an ongoing, dependable, guaranteed income with asset preservation and limited risk.

In other words, legacy planning starts with income planning. It starts with taking care of yourself—exactly what those who love you want you to do!

Retired

As mentioned earlier in the book, life insurance policies can often be issued up to age 80. So even if you're retired, you may be able to create death benefits for your heirs that don't impact your income and spending. If life insurance isn't an option, you can also consider annuities.

Soon to retire

It's critical that you make your legacy planning somewhat separate from your savings. Because if your legacy plan is contingent on you minimizing spending as you age, it could mean that you try to skimp on expenses, leaving you uncomfortable at a time in your life when you shouldn't be.

Under 55 or not planning to retire

Whether you're still in your 30s or in your 50s and planning to never retire, there are still people you may want to provide for with legacy planning. Partners, friends, charities, pets, and so many others can benefit from a well-thought-out legacy plan at any age. If you have loans with cosigners, including student debt, a legacy plan can ensure that they are not on the hook for those costs after you die.

Chapter 9 Checklist

__ Review your legacy planning objectives. Who or what groups do you want to leave something behind for?

__ Look at your real assets and determine who should get which of them.

__ Consider your financial assets and the potential tax issues that might hurt your heirs.

__ Review your life insurance policies, annuities, and other products with death benefits. Are they sufficient for your objectives?

__ Check all your beneficiary designations on policies, accounts, and retirement plans.

Patrick T. Lyman, CAS, CSA, RFC, RHU

Conclusion

A successful retirement plan requires more than just a strategy for saving and growing money, but also a plan for ensuring an adequate source of ongoing income throughout the retiree's golden years.

In *Your 30-Day Retirement Plan*, I created a guide to help you establish your retirement plan. With *The Path to a Stress-Free Retirement,* I've created a guide to help you execute the next phase of your retirement plan without worrying about depleting all your assets before your retirement years are over.

Through reading this book, you've learned about a process and steps to follow to help you build your own personal paycheck for life—something not every retiree or preretiree has.

During my forty-nine years in the financial industry, I've witnessed how significant a crisis the lack of postretirement income planning is. It's shocking when you realize how few retirees in America understand how to build a plan for a predictable and sustainable guaranteed income stream that will last, whether they live to 95 or 105. This is an issue that I believe we all need to pay attention to. Not just so we can secure our own future but so we can help our children and our children's children by taking advantage of solutions that are available now to help solve this most serious problem.

As Lao Tzu once said, "The journey of a thousand miles begins with one step." May the reading of this book be your first and most important step in the lifetime journey of establishing a secure financial future, and may it assist you in making your olden years truly golden.

Glossary

Accumulation: Accumulation is the part of retirement planning that revolves around growing the value of your retirement account(s).

Basis: The initial cost of an investment.

Capital gains: The profit made on the sale of an asset, such as a stock or real estate. Gains are taxed either at long-term rates when they've been held for a year or more, or short-term rates when they've been owned for less than a year.

Compound interest: Interest paid to a principal sum that goes on to earn more interest.

Distribution: Taking funds out of your retirement accounts so you can supplement other income (like Social Security or pension benefits) and pay your living expenses.

Fixed annuity: A contract issued by a life insurance company that guarantees the security of principal paid through a lump sum or periodic payments. Fixed annuities also guarantee a certain rate of interest.

Fixed indexed annuity: Similar to a fixed annuity, but with growth based on the performance of a chosen index.

Front-end load: A sales charge on the purchase of a mutual fund.

Guaranteed minimum withdrawal benefit: An additional rider added to certain annuity contracts that guarantees set lifetime payments.

Immediate annuity: An annuity contract in which a one-time payment is made and guaranteed income starts immediately.

Mutual funds: Funds that invest in a variety of underlying assets such as bonds, stocks, and fixed investments.

Required minimum distribution: A distribution that you are required to begin taking from a Traditional IRA every year starting in the year in which you turn 72 (as of 2020).

Social Security break-even point: The date at which you start taking more out of Social Security than you paid into the system.

Step-up in basis: Resetting the cost basis of assets in an estate to the investment's value on the day the owner passes away.

Stock market indexes: Collections of stocks, such as the Dow Jones Industrial Average and the S&P 500, that allow for the measurement and tracking of performance of the index's portion of the market.

Tax deferral: The ability to delay tax payments to a later date.

Term life insurance: An inexpensive policy designed to offer coverage for a limited period of time. Can often be converted to a whole life policy.

Universal life insurance: A type of permanent life policy with flexible premiums and options for cash value growth. When the cash value performance is tied to subaccounts modeled after stock indexes and has guarantees against losses, it is an index universal life insurance policy.

Variable annuity: Annuity contracts in which you choose subaccounts with a variety of stock and bond investments that are managed by professional money managers, much like mutual funds are.

Whole life insurance: A policy with a guaranteed, fixed premium and death benefit, which also accrues cash values and is designed to offer coverage for your entire life.

Patrick T. Lyman, CAS, CSA, RFC, RHU

Acknowledgments

Writing a book is both a solitary and collaborative endeavor. There are usually many individuals whose input, feedback, and assistance are critically important to the successful completion of the book.

That holds true in the development and completion of *The Path to a Stress-Free Retirement*. My profound thanks to the following individuals who donated their time and feedback and the occasional word of encouragement to help me reach "the end":

Marti Lyman, for beta reading and making content recommendations; Stephen Tepfenhart for beta reading and mentoring me; all my beta readers, including Michael Rafferty, Brendon Murphy, Chris and Bob Scanzaroli, Jeff Maxey, and Diane DiFrancesco.

And last but in no way least, I want to thank my editor and wordsmith extraordinaire, Yolander Prinzel. Her skills as an editor are superb, and her ability to convert thoughts, concepts, and vision into the written word is second to none. Yolander, as the kids say, "You are the bomb!"

The Path to a Stress-Free Retirement

Patrick T. Lyman, CAS, CSA, RFC, RHU

About the Author

Patrick T. Lyman has spent 49 years in the financial industry. As president of Compass Financial Solutions, his mission is to assist individuals and business owners in achieving their retirement income goals with strategies that focus on safety and security. His commitment to his career and clients shows in his dedication, experience, certifications, and industry memberships.

Patrick is a member of the American Society of Financial Services Professionals and the International Association of Registered Financial Consultants. He first qualified for membership in the Million Dollar Round Table in 2005. Membership in this exclusive, premier financial services industry group requires the ability to maintain high service standards focused on enhancing clients' lives, and a steadfast commitment to a strict code of ethics. In 2016 he became a Qualifying and Life member—an honor reserved for those who uphold the group's ethical standards and production requirements for 10 or more consecutive years.

He is also a member of the American Society of Certified Senior Advisors and has been awarded their *Certified Senior Advisor* designation after completing an extensive educational program focused exclusively on issues of financial importance to seniors.

For the last several years, Patrick has regularly conducted educational retirement planning workshops designed to help people determine how to achieve their retirement goals. His commitment to educating people about retirement planning reflects his passion for this issue.

Patrick believes that to be dedicated to his clients, he must also be committed to his community. His efforts to strengthen the financial independence and knowledge of community members is shown through his many educational workshops conducted at various YMCAs in the tri-county area, the Delaware County Police and Firefighters Organization, his past involvement in the Rotary Club of Upper Darby/Lansdowne, and his membership in the Honorable Order of the Kentucky Colonels, a charitable and philanthropic institution founded in 1813.

Patrick currently resides in Drexel Hill, Delaware County. He is married and has three children and four grandchildren. His oldest son is a member of the United States Army Special Forces and has served several tours in Afghanistan and Iraq. As a former president of the Upper Darby/Lansdowne Rotary Club and member in good standing since 2004, Patrick has a long history of activity in a variety of civic and volunteer groups within the community.

www.ingramcontent.com/pod-product-compliance
Lightning Source LLC
Chambersburg PA
CBHW060849220526
45466CB00003B/1303